Make-Ahead Meals
For Busy Moms

Make-Ahead Meals
For Busy Moms

JANE DOIRON

Outskirts Press, Inc.
Denver, Colorado

Make-Ahead Meals for Busy Moms
All Rights Reserved.
Copyright © 2009 Jane Doiron
v13

Cover image by Roger Rivard

http://www.makeaheadmealsforbusymoms.com

Outskirts Press, Inc.
http://www.outskirtspress.com

ISBN: 978-1-4327-2086-5

Library of Congress Control Number: 2009927396

Outskirts Press and the "OP" logo are trademarks belonging to Outskirts Press, Inc.

PRINTED IN THE UNITED STATES OF AMERICA

To Dave, Matthew, and Andrew…I couldn't have made this book without your support. Thank you guys! I love you all so much! To my brother Roger…thank you for taking the pictures for the cover. It was great sharing this experience with you! To my family and friends… my thanks to each one of you for the recipes that you've shared, and for your encouragement and support. Last but not least…I want to thank my friend Kristi Maloney for spending countless hours copywriting, editing, and marketing my first cookbook. You took a huge weight off my shoulders and I am constantly amazed at how much you get accomplished.

Contents

Introduction

I really do love to cook, but it can be a challenge to get dinner on the table after a long, busy day. Never mind the shortage of time, throw in sport schedules, appointments, or just being too tired to cook! So instead of bringing home take-out food or settling on something quick and unhealthy, I've taken my family's favorite meals and turned them into "make-ahead" recipes.

Make-ahead meals can be frozen ahead, assembled ahead, or cooked ahead and reheated. The recipes in this book are a combination of all three. Some of my favorite recipes don't taste their best if they've been frozen, so I've given you the directions to assemble part of the meal the day before. That way, most of the work will be done for you, when you're ready to cook it. Coming home after a busy day and knowing that I can enjoy a home-cooked meal with very little time spent in the kitchen is such a good feeling!

There are many recipes that I try to keep frozen for a quick weeknight meal such as spaghetti sauce with meatballs, sloppy joes, soup, and taco meat. All you have to do is thaw them in the microwave and reheat them. Frozen, marinated meats such as teriyaki chicken and Thai chicken thighs are handy too. Just put them in the refrigerator 24 hours ahead, and they will be thawed and ready to cook at dinnertime the next day.

Make-ahead meals are especially useful around the holidays or when planning a dinner party. It can be very overwhelming when you have to think about cleaning your house and preparing the meal. I find that freezing my cookie dough a few weeks ahead is a real time saver. Think of the time you'll be saving, as you open the freezer and pick out an appetizer, main dish, or dessert that was frozen weeks before, and all you have to do is thaw and heat it!

Once you've tried some of these recipes, you will find that make-ahead meals save you time and money. With a stocked-up freezer full of food that your family enjoys, you're making fewer trips to the grocery store and spending less money on unhealthy prepared or take-out food. By preparing your family's favorite dishes in advance, you'll also control the amount of fat and sodium in your daily meals. Eventually, take-out food will become an occasional treat.

Make-ahead meals are not just for moms who work outside of the home. It's a way of cooking that helps all families, big and small. A little planning is all that's required. Make a meal or two in advance, when you have some extra time. Then you'll be rewarded with quick home-cooked meals, when you really need them.

Helpful Tips

- Invest in an inexpensive vacuum sealer to freeze your meals. They can be found in the freezer storage bag area of the grocery store. You can buy gallon or quart-size bags to go with the model you choose. Using a vacuum sealer makes a noticeable difference in the quality of the food that you freeze. The vacuum sealer removes excess air in the bag eliminating freezer burn. If you use a regular freezer bag, be sure to remove as much air as possible.

- Stock up on freezer bags of different sizes, plastic wrap, and aluminum foil. You can fit more food in your freezer, if you stack your meals flat in freezer bags. Reusable plastic storage containers are great to freeze soups and sauces. Just label them with freezer tape (it sticks better than masking tape).

- Freezing your meals in disposable foil containers comes in handy when you need a meal for a potluck dinner. Not only is your meal prepared in advance, you don't have to worry about getting your dish back.

- Be sure to label your freezer meals. Mark the date, oven temperature, and any other directions, so you won't have to go looking for the recipe when you're in a hurry. This also helps other people in the house, when they are preparing these frozen meals without you. Be sure to mark the number of servings on the package.

- Cool all food completely before you freeze it. Most foods expand upon freezing, so allow enough space between the food and the closure.

- Pack food in quantities that fit your family or lifestyle. I freeze some meals for a family of four and some smaller portions for my college son to take to the dorm. "Flash freeze" food such as meatballs or cookie dough. Lay them out individually in a single layer on a sheet pan. Cover the pan with plastic wrap and freeze just until solid. This will allow you to pack them in a freezer bag without sticking.

- If you like a certain recipe, consider doubling it so you can enjoy half of it now and freeze the other half to enjoy during one of your busy days.

- Buying sale items in bulk is a great way to save money with make-ahead meals. If chicken breast is on sale, make the time to prepare several chicken dishes to freeze.

- If your chicken breast needs to be pounded thin for a recipe, clean and pound it a day ahead and store it in the refrigerator.

- Grate and store fresh cheese in the refrigerator a day ahead. It's a great time saver. If a recipe calls for grated Parmesan cheese, consider buying Parmigiano-Reggiano. It is far superior in flavor to other Parmesan cheeses.

- Dice or chop vegetables a day ahead and store them in the refrigerator.

- When you have the time, buy a freshly baked loaf of French bread and grate the bread in a food processor. Store the bread crumbs in labeled freezer bags and freeze up to 3 months. This will save you time when you need it for a recipe. Just thaw the bread crumbs at room temperature for about 30 minutes before you need them.

- When a recipe calls for buttermilk, use the powdered kind found in the baking aisle of the grocery store. It comes in a 1 lb. container and can be refrigerated up to a year after it's opened. Just follow the directions on the container. There's no need to buy the liquid version, as it won't stay fresh in the refrigerator for very long.

- If you're not much of a wine drinker but like to use a little wine in your recipes, purchase the 4-pack mini bottles of wine in the liquor store and keep them on hand. These are much better than the "cooking" wine, you find near the vinegar section of the grocery store. I prefer Pinot Grigio for cooking. If your recipe calls for Marsala wine, be sure to go to the liquor store and buy fine Marsala wine. It's worth it!

- For more information on freezer storage visit www.whatscookingamerica.net/Information/FreezerChart.htm

Appetizers

Bacon Tomato Mini Cups

Bruschetta

Buffalo Chicken Dip

Crab Melts

Italian Bread Dipping Oil

Italian Sub Spiral Wraps

Mexican Dip

Mini Bacon Quiches

Party Kielbasa

Pizza Bites

Sausage Dip

Shrimp Dip

Stuffed Mushrooms

Sweet and Spicy Meatballs

Taco Dip

Teriyaki Chicken Wings

Warm Crab Dip

Bacon Tomato Mini Cups

A warm appetizer that's especially nice during the winter months!

¾ cup uncooked bacon, chopped into ½-inch pieces
½ cup light mayonnaise
½ cup Swiss cheese, shredded
1 plum tomato, finely chopped
1 teaspoon dried basil
1 (7.5 oz.) tube refrigerated buttermilk biscuits

~A Day Ahead~

Chop the bacon and cook it in a skillet over medium heat until brown and crispy. Remove the bacon to paper towels to drain. Cool completely. In a medium bowl, combine the bacon, mayonnaise, cheese, tomato, and basil. Cover and refrigerate until ready to bake.

~Cooking Directions~

Preheat the oven to 450°F. Separate the biscuit dough into 10 pieces. Cut each piece in half and press one piece into a mini muffin tin like a pie crust. Finish with the rest of the dough in the same manner. Place a tablespoonful of bacon mixture in the center of each cup. Bake for 8 - 9 minutes or until golden brown. Serve warm. Makes 20 appetizers.

You can also cook these ahead, refrigerate them, and warm them up in the oven at 375°F for 3 - 5 minutes.

Bruschetta

Healthy and delicious!

8 plum tomatoes, diced
4 large garlic cloves, minced
½ cup chopped fresh basil leaves
¼ cup extra virgin olive oil
½ teaspoon salt
½ teaspoon pepper
2 (4.75 oz.) bags Panetini Oven Baked Italian Toast (Garlic Parmesan)

~Prepare Up to One Day Ahead~

In a large mixing bowl, combine the tomatoes, garlic, basil, oil, salt, and pepper. Cover and refrigerate until ready to serve. Stir and drain before serving with baked Italian toasts. Serves 8.

Buffalo Chicken Dip

An excellent dip for a football party!

⅓ cup hot sauce

8 oz. cream cheese, softened

½ cup ranch dressing

2 chicken breasts, cooked and shredded

¾ cup celery, diced

1 cup cheddar cheese, shredded

11 oz. bag of bite-size gold tortilla chips

~A Day Ahead~

In a large mixing bowl, mix the hot sauce, cream cheese, and ranch dressing until well blended on low speed. Add the chicken and celery and mix until just combined. Pour the mixture into a 9-inch pie plate and top evenly with the cheddar cheese. Cover with plastic wrap and refrigerate until ready to heat.

~Cooking Directions~

Remove the dip from the refrigerator 30 minutes before heating. Uncover and bake at 350°F for 20 - 30 minutes or until bubbly. Serve hot with tortilla chips or veggies. Serves 8.

Crab Melts

This is a great "make-ahead" appetizer that you can store in your freezer. Just broil as many pieces as you want in less than 10 minutes!

5 oz. Kraft Old English cheese spread
7 tablespoons butter, softened
2 tablespoons mayonnaise
1 large garlic clove, minced
2 cans (6 oz. each) lump crab meat, drained
6 English muffins, split

In a medium mixing bowl, blend the cheese spread, butter, mayonnaise, and garlic on low speed. Add the crab and stir until just combined. On a large sheet pan, place the muffin halves in one single layer. Spread 2 tablespoons of the crab mixture on each half evenly. Cover with plastic wrap and place in the freezer for at least 1 hour. Label and put the cooking directions on 2 large freezer bags; set aside. Cut each frozen muffin slice into quarters on a cutting board and place them in the freezer bags. Seal and freeze up to 3 months. Makes 48 pieces.

~Cooking Directions~

Arrange the frozen appetizers on a sheet pan and place the pan on the upper middle rack in the oven. Broil for 6 - 8 minutes until golden brown.

Italian Bread Dipping Oil

The perfect appetizer to go with an Italian meal!

1½ teaspoons fresh basil, chopped
1½ teaspoons fresh parsley, chopped
¼ teaspoon dried thyme
¼ teaspoon dried oregano
⅛ teaspoon ground black pepper
⅛ teaspoon kosher salt
⅛ to ¼ teaspoon dried rosemary, minced
⅛ teaspoon crushed red pepper flakes
2 tablespoons fresh garlic, minced
½ cup extra virgin olive oil
Fresh Italian bread, sliced

~A Day Ahead~

In a small bowl, combine the basil, parsley, thyme, oregano, pepper, salt, rosemary, and red pepper flakes. Divide the herb mixture into 2 ramekins or small, shallow dishes. Add 1 tablespoon of minced garlic to each ramekin; cover and refrigerate.

~To Serve~

Pour ¼ cup of oil into each ramekin. Stir the oil carefully. Dip small pieces of bread in the dipping oil. Serves 4 - 6.

Italian Sub Spiral Wraps

If you like Italian sub sandwiches, this is a great appetizer for you! To lighten it up, use all ham instead of the mortadella.

2 10-inch thin white wraps
2 tablespoons reduced fat cream cheese with chive and onion
8 slices ham deli meat
4 slices mortadella deli meat
½ cup dill pickles, diced
½ cup plum tomato, diced
2 tablespoons green onion, finely sliced
4 romaine leaves, torn

~Up to 8 Hours Ahead~

Place the wraps on the counter side-by-side. Spread 1 tablespoon of the cream cheese on each wrap (all the way to the edge). Place 4 slices of ham and 2 slices of the mortadella on each wrap (keeping the meat away from the edge by an inch). Sprinkle each wrap with the pickles, tomato, green onions, and romaine. Roll up tightly and secure with 3 or 4 toothpicks. Place the rolls (seam-side down) on a small sheet pan and cover with plastic wrap. Refrigerate until ready to serve. Place the rolls on a cutting board and cut crosswise into 8 spiral pieces. Secure each spiral with a toothpick. Makes 16 spiral wraps.

Mexican Dip

A hearty dip with a little kick!

1 lb. ground beef
1 teaspoon ground chili pepper
1 small onion, finely diced
2 large cloves of garlic, minced
14.5 oz. can diced tomatoes, drained
4½ oz. can green chilies, chopped
1 lb. Velveeta cheese, cubed
Salt and pepper, to taste
Tortilla chips

~A Day Ahead~

In a large nonstick skillet, brown the ground beef with chili pepper, onion, and garlic. Drain the beef mixture. Add the drained tomatoes, green chilies, and cheese. Stir until the cheese is melted. Season with salt and pepper. Pour the mixture into a 9-inch pie plate; cover and refrigerate.

~Cooking Directions~

Reheat in the microwave until bubbly. Serve with tortilla chips.

Mini Bacon Quiches

These cute little quiches are also great for a brunch.

1 package (15 oz.) refrigerated pie pastry
½ lb. bacon, cut into ½-inch pieces
½ cup ricotta cheese
½ cup cheddar cheese, shredded
½ cup Swiss cheese, shredded
1 egg
1 large garlic clove, minced
⅛ teaspoon black ground pepper
2 tablespoons flour

~A Day Ahead~

Remove the pie pastry from the refrigerator and bring to room temperature. Cook the bacon and drain on paper towels. In a medium bowl, mix the bacon, ricotta, cheddar cheese, Swiss cheese, egg, garlic, and pepper.

Sprinkle the counter with flour. Unfold one pie crust and lay flat on flour dusted counter. Use a 2½-inch round cookie cutter to cut out 12 circles of dough. Repeat the same procedure with the 2nd pie pastry. Press each piece of dough into the bottom and sides of a mini muffin cup. Fill each cup evenly with the cheese mixture. Cover tightly with plastic wrap and refrigerate.

~Cooking Directions~

Remove the muffin trays from the refrigerator 30 minutes before cooking. Remove the plastic wrap and bake at 400°F for about 17 minutes or until the cheese is golden brown. Cool on a wire rack. Serve hot. Makes 2 dozen.

Party Kielbasa

For a big party, double the recipe, bake in the oven, and keep warm in a Crock-Pot.

2 lbs. lite Polska kielbasa, sliced ½-inch thin
½ cup vinegar
¼ cup tomato ketchup
¼ cup barbecue sauce
1½ cups light brown sugar, packed

~A Day Ahead~

Mix all of the ingredients together in a large freezer bag. Seal and refrigerate or label and freeze up to 3 months.

~Cooking Directions~

Preheat the oven to 350°F. Place the kielbasa mixture in a 13 x 9 x 2-inch baking dish. Bake for about 50 minutes, turning occasionally. Serves 5 to 6.

Pizza Bites

A delicious appetizer that keeps well in the freezer!

6 English muffins, split
2 plum tomatoes, sliced thin
2¼ cups mozzarella cheese, shredded
½ cup mayonnaise
⅓ cup fresh Parmesan cheese, grated
2½ teaspoons dried basil
2 cloves garlic, minced

Preheat the oven to 375°F. Place 12 English muffin halves on a large baking sheet. Top with one slice of tomato; set aside. In a medium bowl, combine the mozzarella cheese, mayonnaise, Parmesan cheese, basil, and minced garlic. Place a rounded tablespoonful of cheese mixture on top of each tomato. Bake for 3 - 5 minutes. Remove the pan from the oven and flatten and spread the melting cheese so that each muffin half is completely covered. Return to the oven for 9 - 10 minutes until lightly browned. Cool for 20 minutes on a wire rack. Place the muffin halves on a sheet pan, cover with foil, and refrigerate for several hours. If you cut the muffin halves into quarters, after they've been cooked and refrigerated, it will cut very nicely. The pizza bites can stay covered in the refrigerator and can be reheated within the next 24 hours, or you can freeze them for another time. To reheat them from the refrigerator, place them on a sheet pan (on the middle rack) and broil for 6 – 8 minutes until heated through.

~Freezing Directions~

Place the cut-up pizza bites on a large baking sheet and cover with plastic wrap. Freeze for 3 - 4 hours. (This will prevent them from sticking together.) Place the pizza bites in a labeled freezer bag. Freeze up to 2 months.

~Cooking Directions~

Preheat the broiler. Place as many of the frozen pizza bites as you want on a sheet pan, and broil on the middle rack for 8 minutes or until heated through. Makes 48 pieces.

Sausage Dip

Perfect for sausage lovers!

3 hot Italian sausages, casings removed
3 sweet Italian sausages, casings removed
1½ cups Monterey Jack cheese, shredded
1½ cups cheddar cheese, shredded
1 cup ranch dressing
1 small red pepper, finely diced
1 jalapeno, finely diced
Baked pita chips, tortilla chips, or crackers, for dipping

~A Day Ahead~

In a large nonstick skillet over medium heat, break up the sausages into little pieces and cook thoroughly. Drain the fat and set aside to cool. In a medium bowl, add the sausage and the rest of the ingredients; mix well. Cover and refrigerate until you are ready to reheat it.

~Cooking Directions~

Pour the mixture into a 9-inch pie plate and bake at 350°F until bubbly about 20 - 25 minutes. Or reheat small portions in the microwave as you need it. Use your favorite dippers such as baked pita chips, tortilla chips, or crackers. Serves 8.

Shrimp Dip

Easy, quick, and tasty!

8 oz. cream cheese, softened
4 oz. Sau Sea Shrimp Cocktail
2 tablespoons chopped parsley
Bugle chips or crackers

~A Day Ahead~

Mix the cream cheese, Sau Sea Shrimp Cocktail, and parsley in a mixing bowl on low speed. Pour into a serving bowl. Cover and chill in the refrigerator overnight.

Serve cold with Bugle chips or crackers.

*Sau Sea Shrimp Cocktail can be found in the fresh seafood section of the grocery store.

Stuffed Mushrooms

This also makes a great side dish if you love mushrooms.

9 large stuffing mushrooms (save the stems)
⅓ cup mushroom stems, finely chopped
2 tablespoons butter
¼ cup onion, finely chopped
¼ cup green pepper, finely chopped
1 garlic clove, minced
½ cup finely crushed Ritz crackers
¼ cup Parmesan cheese, grated
1 tablespoon fresh parsley, chopped
¼ teaspoon seasoned salt
¼ teaspoon dried oregano
⅔ cup low-sodium chicken broth

~A Day Ahead~

Clean the mushrooms with a paper towel. Chop enough of the stems to equal ⅓ cup. Place the mushroom caps in a 9 x 9 x 2-inch glass dish. Melt the butter in a large nonstick skillet over medium heat. Sauté the stems, onion, green pepper, and garlic until tender. Stir in the cracker crumbs, cheese, parsley, salt, and oregano until well combined. Cool the mixture in a bowl. Stuff the mushrooms, cover the dish with plastic wrap, and refrigerate until ready to bake.

~Cooking Directions~

Remove the dish from the refrigerator 30 minutes before baking. Preheat the oven to 325°F. Remove the plastic wrap and pour the chicken broth into the bottom of the dish to keep the mushrooms from drying out. Bake uncovered for about 25 minutes. Cool for 5 minutes before serving.

Sweet and Spicy Meatballs

Keep the meatballs warm in a Crock-Pot if you are serving them at a party.

Meatballs:

1½ lbs. ground beef, 85% lean

2 eggs

¼ cup milk

½ cup Italian-style bread crumbs

⅓ cup Parmesan cheese, grated

1 tablespoon dried minced onion

2 garlic cloves, minced

½ teaspoon salt

½ teaspoon pepper

Sauce:

12 oz. jar currant jelly

¼ cup water

1 to 2 tablespoons chili garlic sauce (2 tablespoons is very hot!)

2 teaspoons light brown sugar, packed

1 tablespoon cornstarch

~A Day Ahead~

Preheat the oven to 350°F. Mix all of the meatball ingredients together in a large bowl. Form meatballs using a rounded tablespoon of the meatball mixture, and place them on a broiler pan. Bake for 25 minutes. Cool the meatballs, place them in a container, and refrigerate. (You can also freeze the meatballs to make this appetizer at a later date.)

~Cooking Directions~

Take the meatballs out of the refrigerator 30 minutes before cooking. Heat the jelly and water in a large nonstick skillet over medium heat. Stir occasionally until melted. Add the chili garlic sauce, brown sugar, and cornstarch. Whisk until blended. Add the meatballs to the sauce and cook about 15 - 20 minutes (covered) until heated through. Turn and coat the meatballs with the sauce occasionally. Serves 8.

Note: Chili garlic sauce is found in the international aisle with the Asian food.

Taco Dip

A popular dip in my family!

8 oz. cream cheese, softened
16 oz. salsa (medium)
8 oz. shredded taco cheese, divided
10 oz. frozen chopped spinach (drained well)
1 garlic clove, minced

~A Day Ahead~

In a medium mixing bowl, mix the cream cheese, salsa, 1 cup of the taco cheese, spinach, and garlic until well blended. Pour the mixture into a 9-inch pie plate and spread evenly. Sprinkle the remaining taco cheese on top. Cover with plastic wrap and refrigerate.

~Cooking Directions~

Remove the taco dip from the refrigerator about 30 minutes before baking. Remove the plastic wrap and bake at 350°F until bubbly (about 25 minutes). Serve with tortilla chips. Serves 8.

Teriyaki Chicken Wings

Perfect for any occasion!

3 lbs. chicken wings
⅓ cup fresh lemon juice
¼ cup tomato ketchup
¼ cup soy sauce
¼ cup vegetable oil
2 tablespoons light brown sugar, packed
1 garlic clove, minced
¼ teaspoon ground black pepper

~A Day Ahead~

Rinse the chicken and pat them dry with paper towels. Combine the rest of the ingredients in a gallon-size storage bag. Add the chicken and seal well. Refrigerate overnight.

~Cooking Directions~

Preheat the oven to 375°F. Arrange the chicken on a large, foil-covered baking sheet. Bake 1 hour or until nice and brown. Drain the fat halfway through the baking time. Serves 8.

Warm Crab Dip

A rich dip for seafood fans!

2 cans (6 oz. each) lump crabmeat
½ cup mayonnaise
1 cup cheddar cheese, shredded
¼ teaspoon dried minced onion
¼ teaspoon paprika
Cocktail bread or crackers

~A Day Ahead~

In a medium bowl, mix the crabmeat, mayonnaise, cheese, onion, and paprika. Place the mixture in a serving bowl. Cover and refrigerate until ready to heat.

~Cooking Directions~

Warm up the dip in the microwave until heated through; stir well. Serve on your favorite toasted cocktail bread or crackers.

Breakfast and Brunch

Banana Bread

Blueberry Bread

Bran Muffins

Breakfast Burritos

Cinnamon Bread

Coffee Cake with Apple Pie Filling

Cranberry Lemon Bread

Cranberry Scones

Gingerbread Raisin Loaf

Hawaiian Bread

Make-Ahead Coffee Cake

Mini Banana Chocolate Chip Muffins

Mini Pecan Pie Muffins

Overnight Pancake Mix

Pear Bread

Pumpkin Bread

Pumpkin Coffee Cake

Quiche Lorraine

Rhubarb Streusel Bread

Seafood Quiche

Strawberry Bread

Zucchini Apple Bread

Banana Bread

Freeze your extra ripe bananas (unpeeled) in a freezer bag. When you get a craving for banana bread, you just have to thaw them out and they're perfectly ripe for the recipe.

1 cup mashed bananas (use very ripe bananas)
1 cup sugar
½ cup unsalted butter, melted and cooled
2 large eggs
1 teaspoon vanilla extract
1½ cups flour
½ teaspoon salt
1½ teaspoons baking soda
¾ cup walnuts, chopped

Preheat the oven to 350°F. In a large mixing bowl, blend the bananas and sugar together. Add the butter, eggs, and vanilla; mix until combined. On low speed, add the flour, salt, baking soda, and walnuts until completely mixed. Spray 4 mini loaf pans (3½ x 6 x 2) or one (9 x 5 x 3) inch loaf pan with nonstick spray. Pour the batter into the pan(s) evenly. One loaf pan takes about 60 - 70 minutes. Four mini loaf pans take about 25 - 30 minutes. It will be done when an inserted toothpick in the middle comes out clean. Cool on a wire rack.

~Freezing Directions~

When completely cooled, wrap the bread in plastic wrap and place in a labeled freezer bag. Freeze up to 2 months.

Blueberry Bread

If you're a blueberry muffin fan, you'll love this bread!

⅓ cup canola oil
1 egg
1 teaspoon vanilla extract
⅓ cup milk
1½ cups flour
¾ cup sugar
½ teaspoon salt
2 teaspoons baking powder
½ cup walnuts, chopped (optional)
1¼ cup blueberries (mixed with 1 teaspoon flour)

Preheat the oven to 350°F. Spray a 9 x 5 x 3-inch loaf pan with nonstick spray. In a small bowl, blend the oil, egg, vanilla, and milk. In a large mixing bowl, stir the flour, sugar, salt, and baking powder together. Add the liquid ingredients to the dry ingredients and mix on low speed until combined. Add the walnuts and carefully fold in the blueberries. Pour the batter evenly into the prepared pan. Bake for 65 - 70 minutes. It will be done when an inserted toothpick in the middle comes out clean. Cool on a wire rack.

~Freezing Directions~

When the bread is completely cooled, wrap the bread in plastic wrap and place in a labeled freezer bag. Freeze up to 2 months.

Bran Muffins

This makes a great muffin batter that you can make ahead and store in the refrigerator for several days.

2¼ cups original All Bran Cereal (not flakes)
⅔ cup boiling water
1½ cups buttermilk
2 eggs
⅓ cup canola oil
1¾ cups flour
1⅛ cups sugar
1¾ teaspoon baking soda
½ teaspoon salt
1 cup baking raisins

Preheat the oven to 350°F. In a small bowl, combine the bran cereal and water; set aside. In another small bowl, combine the buttermilk, eggs, and oil. In a large mixing bowl, combine the flour, sugar, baking soda, salt, and raisins. Fluff up the cereal mixture with a fork to break into pieces. Add the cereal mixture and the buttermilk mixture to the large bowl. Stir on low speed until just combined. Do not overmix. Spray a muffin pan with nonstick spray. Pour ½ cup of batter into each muffin cup. Bake for about 25 minutes or until an inserted toothpick comes out clean. Cool for 10 minutes in the muffin pan. Then remove the muffins to a wire rack to cool. Makes 12 regular muffins.

~Cooking Directions for Refrigerated Batter~

If the batter has been refrigerated, prepare the muffin pan with nonstick spray, stir up the batter, and add the muffin batter to the muffin pan(s). Let it sit out on the counter for 10 minutes while you heat up the oven to 350°F. Bake for 25 - 27 minutes. Test the muffins with a toothpick.

~Freezing Directions~

When the muffins are completely cooled, place them in labeled freezer bags for up to 2 months.

Breakfast Burritos

Make a batch of these on the weekend and freeze them. Then you can heat them up for breakfast during the week.

1 lb. lean breakfast turkey sausage
1 tablespoon butter
12 eggs
1 cup cheddar cheese, shredded
6 flour toutillas (burrito size)

Heat a large nonstick skillet over medium heat. Remove the casings from the sausage and place them in the skillet. Break the sausages into bite-size pieces with a spatula as they cook. When the sausage is cooked, place it in a bowl and set aside. Carefully remove the grease from the skillet with some paper towels and return to medium heat. Melt the butter in the skillet. Scramble the eggs in a medium bowl. Pour the eggs into the hot skillet and stir frequently until cooked. Remove the skillet from the heat, sprinkle the eggs with cheese and sausage, and stir until well combined. Warm the 6 tortillas between 2 damp paper towels in the microwave for 10 seconds on high. Place 1 cup of the egg filling on each tortilla and roll up like a burrito. Place each burrito seamside down on a cookie sheet, so they won't come apart. Cover all of them with plastic wrap and place in the refrigerator. When they have completely cooled, wrap each burrito in plastic wrap and place in a labeled freezer bag. Freeze up to 1 month.

~Reheat~

Remove the burrito from its packaging and wrap loosely in a paper towel. Microwave the burrito on high until heated through about 1 - 3 minutes. Makes 6.

Cinnamon Bread

Goes great with a cup of coffee!

2 cups flour
1 cup sugar
½ teaspoon baking soda
2 teaspoons baking powder
1½ teaspoons ground cinnamon
1 teaspoon salt
1 cup buttermilk
¼ cup canola oil
2 eggs
1 teaspoon vanilla extract

Streusel Topping:
3 tablespoons sugar
½ teaspoon ground cinnamon
½ cup walnuts, chopped

Preheat the oven to 350°F. Spray two 8 x 4 x 3-inch loaf pans with nonstick spray; set aside. In a large mixing bowl, mix the first 10 ingredients on medium-low speed until blended. Pour the batter into the prepared loaf pans evenly. In a small bowl, mix the streusel ingredients together. Sprinkle the streusel topping over the batter evenly. Bake for 45 minutes or until an inserted toothpick comes out clean. Remove the loaves from the pans and cool on a wire rack.

~Freezing Directions~

When the bread is completely cooled, wrap the bread in plastic wrap and place in a labeled freezer bag. Freeze up to 2 months.

Coffee Cake with Apple Pie Filling

All I can say is…pass me a fork!

12 tablespoons butter, softened

1¼ cups sugar

4 large eggs

8 oz. sour cream

2 teaspoons vanilla extract

2¼ cups flour

1 tablespoon baking powder

¾ teaspoon baking soda

¼ teaspoon salt

Apple Pie Filling:

1 cup sugar

1½ teaspoons cinnamon

6 Granny Smith apples, peeled and sliced into ¼-inch slices

~A Day Ahead~

Preheat the oven to 350°F. Spray a 13 x 9 x 2-inch baking pan with nonstick spray; set aside. Cream the butter and 1¼ cups sugar in a large mixing bowl. On low speed, beat in the eggs, sour cream, and vanilla until combined. In a small bowl, combine the flour, baking powder, baking soda, and salt. Add the flour mixture to the wet ingredients. Mix on low until combined. In a large bowl, mix 1 cup of sugar with the cinnamon. Add the sliced apples to the cinnamon mixture and toss the apples until completely coated. Spread half of the batter evenly into the baking pan. Place two layers of apples on top of the batter. Spread the remaining batter evenly over the apples. (If it doesn't cover the apples completely, that's okay. The batter will spread as it bakes.) Bake for 40 - 45 minutes or until a toothpick inserted into the top cake comes out clean. Cool on a wire rack. Store covered at room temperature. Cut into squares.

Cranberry Lemon Bread

A great lemon flavor with tart, fresh cranberries! Enjoy one loaf now and freeze the other.

¼ cup butter or margarine, softened
1 cup sugar
Lemon zest of 2 lemons
6 oz. lemon yogurt (fruit on the bottom)
2 large eggs
¼ cup fresh lemon juice
2 cups flour
2 teaspoons baking powder
½ teaspoon baking soda
½ teaspoon salt
1 cup fresh cranberries

Preheat the oven to 350°F. Spray two 8 x 4 x 3-inch loaf pans with nonstick spray; set aside. In a large mixing bowl, beat the butter and sugar on medium speed until fluffy. Add the lemon zest, yogurt, eggs, and lemon juice; mix well. In a small bowl, combine the flour, baking powder, baking soda, and salt. Add the dry ingredients and the cranberries to the large mixing bowl and stir on low speed until just combined. Spread the batter evenly into both loaf pans. Bake for 45 - 50 minutes or until a toothpick inserted in the center comes out dry. Remove the bread from each pan and cool on a wire rack.

~Freezing Directions~

When the bread is completely cooled, wrap the bread in plastic wrap and place in a labeled freezer bag. Freeze up to 2 months.

Substitutions for Fresh Cranberries:

1 cup of sweetened dried cranberries, blueberries, or raspberries

Cranberry Scones

A great "freeze-ahead" recipe! Thaw and bake as many scones as you want when you need them.

1 large egg
½ cup whole milk
1 teaspoon vanilla extract
2 cups flour
⅓ cup sugar
2 teaspoons baking powder
¼ teaspoon salt
6 tablespoons cold unsalted butter, cut into ½-inch squares
⅓ cup dried sweetened cranberries
2 teaspoons flour (to dust the countertop)

Egg wash: 1 egg plus 1 tablespoon whole milk, blended
1 tablespoon sugar

In a small bowl, combine 1 egg, ½ cup milk, and vanilla; set aside. In a large mixing bowl, combine the flour, sugar, baking powder, and salt. With the mixer on low-medium speed, add the butter and mix until the mixture has very small crumbs. Add the wet ingredients on low speed. Stir in the cranberries. Lightly dust the countertop with 2 teaspoons of flour. Place the dough on top of the flour and knead the dough a few times. Flatten the dough into a circle that is 1 inch thick. Cut the dough like a pie, giving you 8 equal wedges. Place the wedges on a sheet pan, cover with plastic wrap, and freeze for 3 - 4 hours. Place the frozen scones in a labeled freezer bag and include the following directions:

Cover a sheet pan with parchment paper. Place the frozen scones on top and thaw at room temperature for 30 minutes. Brush the tops with the egg wash and sprinkle with sugar. Bake for 20 minutes at 375°F. The scones are done when a toothpick inserted in the center comes out clean. Serve warm or at room temperature. This recipe makes 8 scones and can be frozen up to 2 months.

Gingerbread Raisin Loaf

If you like gingerbread, you'll love this easy, quick bread. Use moist baking raisins if possible. It makes a big difference. This makes two loaves that freeze well.

1¾ cups all-purpose flour
¾ cup white whole wheat flour
2 teaspoons baking powder
½ teaspoon baking soda
1½ teaspoons ground ginger
¼ teaspoon salt
½ teaspoon ground cloves
1 teaspoon ground cinnamon
¼ teaspoon ground nutmeg
1 cup 1% low-fat milk
½ cup molasses
¼ cup canola oil
2 large eggs
¾ cup packed light brown sugar
½ to ¾ cup baking raisins

Preheat the oven to 350°F. Spray two 8 x 4 x 3-inch loaf pans with nonstick spray; set aside. In a large mixing bowl, combine the flour, baking powder, baking soda, ginger, salt, cloves, cinnamon, and nutmeg. In a small bowl, combine the milk, molasses, oil, eggs, brown sugar, and raisins until well blended. Add the wet ingredients to the large mixing bowl. Stir until just combined. Pour the batter equally into both loaf pans. Add a few extra raisins on the top of each loaf. (Because the batter is so thin, many raisins sink to the bottom when cooking.) Bake for 47 - 50 minutes or until a toothpick inserted in the center comes out dry. Remove the loaves from the pan and cool on a wire rack.

~Freezing Directions~

When the bread is completely cooled, wrap in plastic wrap and place in a labeled freezer bag. Freeze up to 2 months.

Hawaiian Bread

This is a delicious, colorful bread to give at Christmastime!

1¾ cup flour
2 teaspoons baking powder
½ teaspoon salt
¾ cup sugar
1 egg
5 tablespoons butter, softened
1 cup bananas, mashed
¾ cup macadamia nuts, chopped
10 oz. jar maraschino cherries, quartered

Preheat the oven to 350°F. Spray two 8 x 4 x 3-inch loaf pans with nonstick spray; set aside. In a small bowl, combine the flour, baking powder, and salt; set aside. In a large mixing bowl, combine the sugar, egg, and butter on medium speed until well blended. Add the bananas and mix well. On low speed, mix in the flour mixture until combined. Stir in the nuts and cherries. Divide the batter equally into the two loaf pans. Bake for 50 minutes or until a toothpick inserted in the center comes out clean. Cool the loaves on a wire rack.

~Freezing Directions~

Be sure the bread is completely cool before you wrap it well with plastic wrap. Place in a labeled freezer bag and freeze up to 2 months.

Make-Ahead Coffee Cake

This is the perfect recipe for brunch! Assemble it in the evening and bake it fresh in the morning!

Cake:

1½ sticks unsalted butter, softened

3 large eggs

1½ cups sour cream

1 tablespoon vanilla extract

2¼ cups flour

1¼ cups sugar

2 teaspoons baking powder

1 teaspoon baking soda

½ teaspoon salt

Streusel:

⅓ cup light brown sugar, packed

⅓ cup sugar

2 tablespoons flour

1 teaspoon cinnamon

⅔ cup walnuts, chopped

~A Day Ahead~

Spray a 10 x 12 x 2-inch baking pan with nonstick spray; set aside. In a large mixing bowl, cream the butter and mix in the eggs, sour cream, and vanilla. In a medium bowl, combine the flour, sugar, baking powder, baking soda, and salt. Add the dry ingredients to the wet ingredients and mix on low speed until combined. Increase the speed to medium-high for 2 minutes. Pour evenly into the prepared pan. Cover with plastic wrap and refrigerate until ready to bake. Combine the streusel ingredients in a small bowl, cover tightly, and store at room temperature.

~In the Morning~

Remove the pan from the refrigerator 30 minutes before baking. Preheat the oven to 350°F. Remove the plastic wrap and sprinkle the streusel evenly over the batter. Bake for about 45 minutes or until a toothpick inserted in the center comes out clean. Cool on a wire rack.

Mini Banana Chocolate Chip Muffins

An easy recipe that kids enjoy!

½ cup butter, softened
1 cup sugar
2 eggs
2 medium-size, very ripe bananas, mashed
2 cups flour
1 teaspoon baking soda
½ cup walnuts or pecans, chopped
½ cup mini chocolate chips

Preheat the oven to 350°F. Coat 24 mini muffin cups with nonstick spray. (There will be enough batter to make a little more than 24.) In a large bowl, cream the butter and sugar together. Add the eggs, beating until smooth. Add the bananas and mix until combined. In a small bowl, mix the flour and the baking soda; add to the creamed mixture. Fold in the nuts and chocolate chips. Fill each muffin cup with the batter above the rim. Bake for about 15 minutes or until a toothpick inserted in the center comes out dry. Cool the muffins in the pan for about 5 minutes, before you place the muffins on a wire rack to cool.

~Freezing Directions~

Cool completely, place in a labeled freezer bag, and freeze up to 2 months.

Mini Pecan Pie Muffins

You won't find an easier muffin recipe than this. Perfect for a baby or wedding shower brunch!

1 cup light brown sugar, packed
1 cup pecans, chopped
½ cup flour
⅔ cup butter, melted
2 eggs, beaten

Spray 20 mini muffin cups with nonstick spray; set aside. Preheat the oven to 350°F. In a medium bowl, mix all of the ingredients together. Spoon the batter into the muffin cups evenly. Bake for 18 - 20 minutes. The edges will be crispy. Do not overcook. Remove the muffins and cool on a wire rack.

~Freeze~

When the muffins are completely cool, place the muffins in a labeled freezer bag and freeze up to 2 months.

Overnight Pancake Mix

Enjoy these pancakes for breakfast, lunch, or dinner. It's a real time-saver!

2 cups flour
½ cup sugar
2½ teaspoons baking powder
2 teaspoons baking soda
2 cups whole milk
½ cup vegetable oil
2 eggs
Vegetable oil (as needed) for the skillet

~A Day Ahead~

In a large bowl, combine the flour, sugar, baking powder, baking soda, milk, ½ cup oil, and eggs. Cover and refrigerate overnight.

~Cooking Directions~

In the morning, remove the bowl from the refrigerator 30 minutes before cooking. Heat a large nonstick skillet over medium heat and add a tablespoon of oil. When the pan is hot, turn it down slightly. For each pancake, pour ¼ cup of the batter onto the center of the skillet. Tilt the pan slightly in every direction to get the pancake to spread larger and thinner. When the edges are brown and there are lots of bubbles on the surface of the batter, flip the pancake carefully. Cook until lightly brown on each side. You will need to add oil to the pan as necessary. Makes 12 five-inch pancakes.

Pear Bread

This is one of my favorites! It's spicy, moist, and keeps well for days.

3 cans (15 oz. each) lite pear halves in extra light syrup, drained
½ cup canola oil
3 eggs
3¼ cups flour
1 cup sugar
3 teaspoons cinnamon
½ teaspoon ground cloves
½ teaspoon nutmeg
1 teaspoon baking soda
1 teaspoon baking powder
½ teaspoon salt
1 cup chopped walnuts

Preheat the oven to 350°F. Spray two 8 x 4 x 3-inch loaf pans with nonstick spray; set aside. In a large mixing bowl, mash the pears with a potato masher. Stir in the oil and eggs. In a medium bowl, combine the rest of the ingredients. Slowly add the dry ingredients to the pear mixture on low speed until thoroughly combined. Pour the batter equally into the loaf pans. Bake for 70 - 75 minutes or until a toothpick inserted in the middle comes out clean. Cool on a wire rack.

~Freezing Directions~

When completely cooled, wrap the bread in plastic wrap and place in a labeled freezer bag. Freeze up to 2 months.

Pumpkin Bread

This bread is so good! I can't get through the Thanksgiving holiday without it!

3½ cups flour

2 teaspoons baking soda

1 teaspoon cinnamon

3 cups sugar

1½ teaspoons salt

1 teaspoon nutmeg

1 teaspoon allspice

¼ teaspoon ground ginger

2 cups canned pumpkin

4 eggs, well beaten

1 cup canola oil

⅔ cup water

1 cup walnuts, chopped

Preheat the oven to 350°F. Spray three 9 x 5 x 3-inch loaf pans with nonstick spray. Coat the inside of each pan with a tablespoon of flour. Tap out the excess flour; set aside. Combine all of the ingredients in a large mixing bowl. Divide the batter equally into the 3 pans. Bake for 1 hour or until toothpick inserted in the center of bread comes out clean. Cool on a wire rack.

~Freezing Directions~

When completely cooled, wrap the bread in plastic wrap, place in a labeled freezer bag, and freeze up to 2 months.

Pumpkin Coffee Cake

A great recipe for Thanksgiving brunch or dessert!

½ cup butter, softened

1½ cup sugar

15 oz. can pumpkin

3 large eggs

2½ cups flour

2 teaspoons baking powder

1 tablespoon cinnamon

1½ teaspoons ground ginger

½ teaspoon ground nutmeg

¼ teaspoon cloves

½ teaspoon salt

Streusel topping:

¼ cup flour

¼ cup sugar

¼ cup light brown sugar, packed

½ teaspoon cinnamon

2 tablespoons butter, melted

⅓ cup walnuts, chopped

~A Day Ahead~

Preheat the oven to 350°F. Spray the inside of a tube or Bundt pan with nonstick spray; set aside. In a large mixing bowl, beat the butter and sugar on medium speed until well blended. Add the pumpkin and eggs and mix thoroughly. In a medium bowl, combine the flour, baking powder, cinnamon, ginger, nutmeg, cloves, and salt. Add the flour mixture to the pumpkin mixture. Mix on medium speed until combined. Pour the batter into the prepared pan. Prepare the streusel topping: In a small bowl combine the flour, sugars, cinnamon, melted butter, and walnuts. Sprinkle the streusel over the cake batter. Bake for 50 - 55 minutes or until a toothpick comes out clean. Cool on a wire rack about 15 minutes. Slide a knife around the pan so that the cake doesn't stick when removing it. Invert the cake onto a plate. Then invert the cake onto another plate, so that the streusel is on the top. Cool completely. Cover and store at room temperature.

Quiche Lorraine

(Shown on the back cover.) A Creamy, rich, comfort food that tastes great reheated!

One 9-inch frozen pie crust, thawed
4 eggs
1½ cups half-and-half cream
10 slices store-bought, pre-cooked bacon, cut into ½-inch pieces
1 cup mild cheddar or Gruyere cheese, shredded
¼ teaspoon pepper

~A Day Ahead~

Preheat the oven to 375°F. In a large bowl, lightly beat the eggs with half-and-half. Stir in the bacon, cheese, and pepper. Pour into the pie shell. Place the quiche on a rimmed baking sheet and bake for 40 minutes or until a toothpick inserted in the center comes out clean. Cool on a wire rack. Cover and refrigerate.

~Cooking Directions~

Reheat the quiche in the microwave.

Rhubarb Streusel Bread

A great way to use up the rhubarb in your garden!

1½ cups light brown sugar, packed
½ cup canola oil
1 egg
1 cup buttermilk
1 teaspoon vanilla extract
2½ cups flour
1 teaspoon baking soda
½ teaspoon salt
1¼ cup rhubarb, diced
¾ cup walnuts, chopped

Topping:
½ cup sugar
¼ teaspoon ground cinnamon
1 tablespoon cold butter, cut into 4 pieces

~A Day Ahead~

Preheat the oven to 350°F. Spray two 8 x 4 x 3-inch loaf pans with nonstick spray. In a large mixing bowl, beat the brown sugar and oil together. Add the egg; mix well. Slowly beat in the buttermilk and vanilla. In a medium bowl, combine the flour, baking soda, and salt. Add the flour mixture to the wet ingredients and stir on low speed until just combined. Fold in the rhubarb and nuts. Pour the batter equally into the two loaf pans.

For the topping: Combine the sugar, cinnamon, and butter in a small mixing bowl. Beat on medium-high speed until crumbly. Sprinkle the topping evenly over the batter. Bake for 55 - 60 minutes or until a toothpick inserted in the center comes out clean. Cool for 5 minutes in the pan. Then cool the loaves on a wire rack. Enjoy one loaf today and freeze the other!

~Freezing Directions~

When completely cooled, wrap the bread in plastic wrap and place in a labeled freezer bag. Freeze up to 2 months.

Seafood Quiche

A great recipe for breakfast, lunch, or dinner!

9-inch deep dish frozen pie crust, thawed
1 can (6 oz.) lump crabmeat, drained
1 can (4 oz.) medium shrimp, drained
1 cup mild cheddar or Monterey Jack cheese, shredded
2 tablespoons green onion, finely sliced
4 eggs
1½ cup half-and-half cream
¼ teaspoon pepper

~A Day Ahead~

Preheat the oven to 375°F. Place the crabmeat and shrimp evenly in the bottom of the pie shell. Top with cheese and green onion. In a small bowl, whisk the eggs, half-and-half, and pepper. Pour the egg mixture over everything in the pie. Place the pie on a rimmed baking sheet. Bake for about 40 minutes or until a toothpick inserted in the center comes out clean. Cool on a wire rack. Cover and refrigerate.

~Cooking Directions~

Reheat the quiche in the microwave.

Strawberry Bread

This moist, delicious recipe makes 3 loaves. One for now, one to give away, and one to freeze!

3¼ cups flour
1¾ cups sugar
½ teaspoon cinnamon
½ teaspoon salt
1 teaspoon baking soda
16 oz. frozen sliced strawberries with sugar, thawed (including the juice)
3 large eggs, slightly beaten
1 cup canola oil

Preheat the oven to 350°F. Spray three 8 x 4 x 3-inch loaf pans with nonstick spray; set aside. Mix the flour, sugar, cinnamon, salt, and baking soda in a large mixing bowl. Add the strawberries on low speed. (You don't want big chunks of strawberry in the bread.) Mix in the eggs and the oil until well combined. Pour the batter equally into the 3 loaf pans. Bake for 60 - 70 minutes or until a toothpick inserted in the center comes out clean. Remove the bread from the pan. Cool on a wire rack.

~Freezing Directions~

When the bread is completely cooled, wrap the bread in plastic wrap and place in a labeled freezer bag. Freeze up to 2 months.

Zucchini Apple Bread

A tasty version of the classic zucchini bread!

5 eggs

1½ cups canola oil

2 cups sugar

1 cup light brown sugar, packed

2 teaspoons vanilla extract

4 cups flour

1 tablespoon baking soda

1 tablespoon ground cinnamon

½ teaspoon ground nutmeg

½ teaspoon salt

2 cups shredded zucchini, excess moisture removed with paper towels

1 cup peeled, grated apples (Cortland or Granny Smith)

1½ cups walnuts, chopped

Preheat the oven to 350°F. Spray three 8 x 4 x 3-inch loaf pans with nonstick spray; set aside. In a medium bowl, beat the eggs, oil, sugars, and vanilla on medium speed until blended. In a large mixing bowl, combine the flour, baking soda, cinnamon, nutmeg, and salt. Add the egg mixture to the large bowl and mix on low speed until just combined. Stir in the zucchini, apples, and walnuts. Pour the batter equally into the 3 loaf pans. Bake for 60 - 70 minutes or until a toothpick inserted in the center comes out clean. Remove the bread from the pan and cool on a wire rack.

~Freezing Directions~

When completely cooled, wrap the bread in plastic wrap and place in a labeled freezer bag. Freeze up to 2 months.

Dessert

Angel Food Cake
Big Ginger Cookies
Blueberry Squares
Brownie Cookies
Brownies
Cherry Bars
Chocolate Chip Blondies
Chocolate Chip Cookies
Chocolate Fudge
Chocolate Torte
Christmas Bark
Date Bars
Flaky Pie Crust
Freezable Lemon Bars
Gingerbread
Granola Bars

Italian Cookies
Lemonade Cake
Lemon Lush
Macadamia Nut Cookies
Maple Walnut Fudge
Mini Cheesecakes
Oatmeal Cookies
Peanut Butter Choc. Chip Crackles
Peanut Butter Fudge
Peanut Butter Kiss Cookies
Penuche Fudge
Pound Cakes
Pumpkin Pie
Snickerdoodle Cookies
Tiramisu
Walnut Tassies

Angel Food Cake

Serve this light and airy cake with sweetened strawberries and whipped cream.

1 cup flour
1½ cup confectioner's sugar
¼ teaspoon salt
12 egg whites
1 teaspoon cream of tartar
2 teaspoons vanilla extract
1 cup sugar

~A Day Ahead~

Preheat the oven to 375°F. In a medium bowl, combine the flour, confectioner's sugar, and salt. In a large mixing bowl, beat the egg whites, cream of tartar, and vanilla until foamy on medium speed. Slowly add the sugar to the egg whites. Increase to high speed and beat until stiff peaks form. Gently fold in the flour mixture a little at a time. Do not overmix. Pour the batter into an ungreased tube pan and spread it gently. Bake for 30 - 33 minutes, or when the top springs back when lightly tapped. Remove the cake from the oven and immediately turn the cake upside down, hanging over a bottle or funnel, until completely cooled. Use a sharp knife to cut between the cake and the pan, so that you can remove it without sticking. Place the cake on a plate. Cover with plastic wrap and store at room temperature.

Big Ginger Cookies

This is a great cookie for bake sales, cookie swaps, or gifts for Christmas. They're spicy, thick, and delicious!

1½ cups shortening

2 cups sugar

2 eggs

½ cup molasses

4½ cups flour

3½ teaspoons ground ginger

2 teaspoons baking soda

1½ teaspoons ground cinnamon

1 teaspoon ground cloves

½ teaspoon nutmeg

¼ teaspoon salt

½ cup sugar (to coat the cookie dough)

In a large mixing bowl, beat the shortening and sugar on medium speed until fluffy. Add the eggs and molasses; mix well. In a medium bowl, combine the flour, ginger, baking soda, cinnamon, cloves, nutmeg, and salt. Slowly add the dry ingredients to the shortening mixture and beat on low speed until combined. Place a layer of parchment paper on a large cookie sheet pan. Shape the dough into large balls using a level ⅛ cup of cookie dough. Roll each ball in sugar and place about 2 inches apart on the cookie sheet. Bake at 350°F for about 10 - 12 minutes. Do not overbake or they will not be soft and chewy. The cookie will look uncooked in the cracks but will set up upon cooling. Cool for a few minutes on the sheet pan. Then transfer to wire racks to cool. Makes about 23 large cookies.

~Freezing Directions for Uncooked Dough~

Shape the dough into balls and roll in the sugar. Place them on a sheet pan and cover with plastic wrap. Freeze for 2 - 3 hours. Place the frozen dough in a labeled freezer bag. Write the cooking directions on the bag. Freeze up to 2 months.

~Thawing Out the Dough on Baking Day~

Cover a large sheet pan with parchment paper. Place the frozen cookie dough on the sheet pan about 2 inches apart. Thaw the dough at room temperature for 30 - 45 minutes. Preheat the oven to 350°F and bake for about 12 minutes. Cool on a wire rack.

Blueberry Squares

A nice blueberry flavor without being too sweet!

Dough:
¾ cup sugar
3 cups flour
1 teaspoon baking powder
1 cup cold butter, cut into ½-inch squares
1 egg

Filling:
3½ cups small blueberries (see note)
⅓ cup sugar
1 tablespoon cornstarch

Note: If using frozen blueberries, thaw them at room temperature for 30 minutes before mixing them with the other filling ingredients.

~A Day Ahead~

Preheat the oven to 375°F. Spray a 13 x 9 x 2-inch baking pan with nonstick spray. In a large mixing bowl, combine the ¾ cup of sugar, flour, and baking powder. While the mixer is on low speed, add the butter pieces to the flour mixture. When all the butter has been added, increase the speed to medium-high to blend the ingredients and form a crumbly mixture. On medium speed, add the egg until thoroughly combined. Press half of the dough into the prepared pan. In a medium bowl, combine the blueberries, ⅓ cup of sugar, and cornstarch. Spread the blueberry mixture over the crust. Sprinkle the remaining dough over the top, breaking up any big chunks of dough. Bake for 45 minutes or until the center is cooked through. Cool on a wire rack. Cut into squares.

Brownie Cookies

If you like brownies, you'll love this cookie!

½ cup butter, softened

¾ cup light brown sugar, packed

½ cup sugar

1 egg

½ cup sour cream

1 teaspoon vanilla extract

1¾ cups flour

½ cup unsweetened baking cocoa

1 teaspoon baking powder

½ teaspoon baking soda

¼ teaspoon salt

¾ cup semisweet chocolate chips

¾ cup peanut butter chips

In a large mixing bowl, cream the butter and sugars. Add the egg, sour cream, and vanilla; mix well. In a medium bowl, combine the flour, cocoa, baking powder, baking soda, and salt. Gradually add the dry ingredients to the creamed mixture. Mix in the chips on low speed. If baking now, preheat the oven to 350°F and prepare a large sheet pan with parchment paper. Drop the cookie dough by rounded tablespoonfuls about 2 inches apart. Bake for 12 - 14 minutes or until set. Cool for 5 minutes on the cookie sheet. Transfer the cookies to a cooling rack. Makes about 46 cookies.

~Freezing Directions for Uncooked Dough~

Cover a large cookie sheet with wax paper. Drop the cookie dough by rounded tablespoonfuls about ½-inch apart. Cover with plastic wrap and freeze the dough for 3 - 4 hours or until frozen. Place the frozen dough in a labeled freezer bag. Write the cooking directions on the bag. Freeze up to 2 months.

~Thawing Out the Dough on Baking Day~

Cover a large cookie sheet with parchment paper and place the frozen cookie dough on it about 2 inches apart. Thaw the dough at room temperature for 30 - 45 minutes. Preheat the oven to 350°F and bake as directed.

Brownies

Everybody needs a good brownie recipe on hand!

1½ cups flour
¾ cup unsweetened cocoa
¾ teaspoon salt
3 large eggs
1¾ cups sugar
1 teaspoon vanilla extract
½ cup butter, softened
¼ cup shortening
1 cup walnuts, chopped (optional)

~A Day Ahead~

Preheat the oven to 350°F. Spray an 11 x 7 x 2-inch baking dish with nonstick spray; set aside. In a small bowl, combine the flour, cocoa, and salt. In a large mixing bowl, beat the eggs, sugar, vanilla, butter, and shortening on medium speed until smooth. Add the flour mixture and walnuts to the large mixing bowl. Mix on low speed until thoroughly combined. Pour the batter evenly into the prepared pan. Bake for 30 - 35 minutes or until a toothpick inserted in the center comes out clean or with a few dry crumbs attached. Cool the pan on a wire rack. Cover and store at room temperature. Cut into bars.

Cherry Bars

An old childhood favorite of mine! If you're fond of strawberries, try the canned strawberry pie filling instead of the cherry. Either way, you can't lose.

1 cup butter, softened
2 cups sugar
4 large eggs
1½ teaspoons vanilla extract
3 cups flour
¾ teaspoon salt
½ teaspoon baking powder
21 oz. can cherry pie filling

~A Day Ahead~

Preheat the oven to 350°F. Spray a 13 x 9 x 2-inch baking pan with nonstick spray; set aside. In a large mixing bowl, cream the butter and sugar. Add the eggs and vanilla and beat until smooth. In a medium bowl, combine the flour, salt, and baking powder. Add the flour mixture to the creamed mixture. Mix until smooth. Spread half of the batter into the pan evenly. Spread the cherry filling on top. With the remaining batter, drop teaspoons of batter all over the cherry filling. Bake for 50 - 55 minutes or until a toothpick comes out clean. Cool completely on a wire rack. Cut into bars. Cover and store at room temperature.

Chocolate Chip Blondies

If you're in the mood for a chocolate chip cookie, these will hit the spot!

½ cup sugar
1 cup light brown sugar, packed
½ cup butter, melted
2 large eggs
1 teaspoon vanilla extract
1½ cups flour
½ teaspoon baking powder
½ teaspoon salt
1½ cups semisweet chocolate morsels

~A Day Ahead~

Preheat the oven to 350°F. Spray a 13 x 9 x 2-inch baking pan with nonstick spray; set aside. In a large bowl, beat the sugars, butter, eggs, and vanilla until well blended. In a small bowl, combine the flour, baking powder, and salt. Add the dry ingredients to the large mixing bowl and mix on low speed until combined. Stir in the chocolate chips. Pour the batter into the pan and spread evenly. Bake for 22 - 24 minutes or until a toothpick inserted in the center comes out clean. Cool the pan on a wire rack. Cool completely before cutting into bars. Cover and store at room temperature.

Chocolate Chip Cookies

This is definitely a family favorite! The pudding mix keeps them moist for days.

1 cup butter, softened
¾ cup light brown sugar, packed
¼ cup sugar
1 box (3.4 oz.) instant French vanilla pudding mix
2 eggs
1 teaspoon vanilla extract
2⅓ cups flour
1 teaspoon baking soda
12 oz. semisweet chocolate morsels
1 cup walnuts, chopped

Preheat the oven to 350°F. In a large mixing bowl, cream the butter, sugars, and pudding mix. On low speed, add the eggs and vanilla. In a medium bowl, combine the flour and baking soda. Gradually add the dry ingredients to the creamed mixture. Mix in the chocolate chips and walnuts. Place parchment paper on a large cookie sheet. Drop the cookie dough by rounded tablespoonful about 2 inches apart. Bake for 8 - 10 minutes or until golden brown around the edges. Cool for 3 - 5 minutes on the sheet pan. Then transfer the cookies to a cooling rack. Makes 5 dozen small cookies.

~Freezing Directions for Uncooked Dough~

Cover a large cookie sheet with wax paper. Drop the cookie dough by rounded tablespoonful about an inch apart on the sheet pan. Cover with plastic wrap and freeze 3 - 4 hours. Place the dough in a labeled freezer bag. Write the cooking directions on the bag. Freeze up to 2 months.

~Thawing Out the Dough on Baking Day~

Cover a large cookie sheet with parchment paper and place the frozen cookie dough on it about 2 inches apart. Thaw at room temperature for 30 - 45 minutes. Preheat the oven to 350°F and bake the cookies for about 10 minutes or until the edges are golden brown.

Chocolate Fudge

Fudge freezes easily, as long as you freeze it whole and wrap it well. Thaw it out completely, before you cut it into pieces.

2 cups sugar
⅔ cup evaporated milk
14 regular marshmallows
½ cup butter
¼ teaspoon salt
6 oz. semisweet chocolate morsels
1 cup walnuts, chopped
1 teaspoon vanilla extract

Line an 8 x 8 x 2-inch baking dish with plastic wrap. Combine the sugar, milk, marshmallows, butter, and salt in a 2-quart saucepan. Stir constantly over medium heat until it boils. Stir for 5 more minutes and remove from the stove. Stir in the chocolate chips until they melt. Stir in the walnuts and vanilla and pour the fudge into the prepared pan. It will take several hours to set. Cool completely before cutting. Pull up on the plastic wrap and lift the fudge out of the pan. Peel away the wrap and place the fudge on a cutting board. Cut into squares.

~Freezing Directions~

Wrap the whole piece of fudge in plastic wrap and place in a labeled freezer bag. Freeze up to 2 months.

Chocolate Torte

A rich, decadent dessert you're sure to love!

2 cups Vanilla Wafer reduced fat cookies, crushed
5 tablespoons butter, melted
⅔ cup walnuts, chopped
8 oz. Neufchatel cheese, softened
1 cup confectioner's sugar
½ cup peanut butter
4 cups whipped topping, divided
3 cups whole milk
2 packages (3.9 oz. each) instant chocolate pudding mix

~A Day Ahead~

Preheat the oven to 350°F. In a medium bowl, combine the cookie crumbs, butter, and walnuts. Press into an ungreased 13 x 9 x 2-inch baking pan. Bake the crust for 8 - 10 minutes or until lightly browned. Cool on a wire rack. In a large mixing bowl, beat the Neufchatel cheese, sugar, and peanut butter on medium speed until smooth. Fold in 2 cups of the whipped topping. Spread evenly over the crust. In a medium mixing bowl, beat the milk and pudding mix on low-medium speed until thickened. Spread evenly over the cream cheese layer. Spread the remaining whipped topping on top; cover and refrigerate. Keep refrigerated until ready to serve. Cut into squares.

Christmas Bark

This makes a great gift for the holidays! Place them in a Christmas cellophane bag and wrap it with a pretty bow.

35 saltine crackers
1 stick of butter or margarine
½ cup sugar
12 oz. bag semi-sweet chocolate chips

Topping choices:
Heath Toffee Bits
Walnuts, finely chopped

~A Day Ahead~

Preheat the oven to 400°F. Line a 13 x 9 x 2-inch sheet pan with foil. Lay the crackers on the pan (5 rows of crackers with 7 crackers in each row). In a small saucepan over medium heat, cook the butter and sugar together until bubbly, stirring occasionally. Pour the butter mixture over the saltines evenly, and bake for 5 minutes. Remove the pan from the oven and sprinkle the chocolate chips evenly over the top. Bake for 2 minutes. Remove the pan from the oven and use a knife to smooth and spread the melted chocolate evenly. Sprinkle Heath Toffee Bits or walnuts over the chocolate. Set aside to cool. Refrigerate for one hour. Break the crackers into pieces. For gift giving, place the bark in holiday cellophane bags and seal the bag with a bow or twisty tie. Or keep the bark covered at room temperature.

Date Bars

A good old-fashioned classic!

8 oz. bag pitted dates, chopped
1 tablespoon sugar
¾ cup water
⅓ cup walnuts, chopped
1¼ cup flour
½ teaspoon salt
½ teaspoon baking soda
1½ cups quick-cooking oats
1 cup light brown sugar, packed
½ cup butter, softened (cut into 8 pieces)

~A Day Ahead~

Preheat the oven to 350°F. Spray a 9 x 9 x 2-inch baking dish with nonstick spray. In a medium saucepan, cook the dates, sugar, and water over medium heat. Stir until the mixture thickens, about 4 - 5 minutes. Add the walnuts and set aside to cool. In a large mixing bowl, combine the flour, salt, baking soda, oats, and brown sugar. On medium speed, mix in the butter until crumbly. Press half of the oat mixture into the baking pan. Spread the date mixture evenly on top. Pour the rest of the oat mixture evenly over the dates and pat it down lightly. Bake for 30 minutes until lightly browned. Cool on a wire rack. Cut into bars and cover at room temperature.

~Freeze~

Wrap and freeze individual bars in plastic wrap and place them in a labeled freezer bag. Freeze up to 1 month

Flaky Pie Crust

An easy "make-ahead" recipe!

4 cups flour
2 teaspoons salt
1½ cups shortening
1 teaspoon white vinegar
2 tablespoons milk
½ cup hot water

~A Day Ahead~

Combine the flour and salt in a small bowl. In a large mixing bowl, mix the shortening, vinegar, milk, and hot water on low speed until smooth. Add the flour mixture to the wet ingredients and stir on low speed until it comes together to form a ball. Roll out half the dough between two sheets of wax paper. Wrap well with plastic wrap and lay flat in the refrigerator. Roll out the other half of the dough between two sheets of wax paper. Wrap well with plastic wrap and lay flat on top of the other pie crust in the refrigerator.

Take the pie crusts out of the refrigerator 30 minutes before you need them.

Freezable Lemon Bars

A tasty "make-ahead" dessert for unexpected company!

1½ cups graham cracker crumbs

⅓ cup sugar

5 tablespoons butter, melted

3 egg yolks

14 oz. can sweetened condensed milk

½ cup fresh lemon juice

12 oz. tub of frozen whipped topping, thawed serving

Preheat the oven to 325°F. In a small mixing bowl, combine the crumbs, sugar, and butter. Press this mixture firmly in a 9 x 9 x 2-inch ungreased foil pan. In a small mixing bowl, beat the egg yolks, condensed milk, and lemon juice for one minute on low-medium speed. Pour over the crust evenly. Bake for about 30 minutes or until firm. Cool completely before spreading the whipped topping over it. Cover well with plastic wrap, place in a large freezer bag and freeze up to a month. Let stand at room temperature 30 minutes before serving. Cut into bars.

This can also be refrigerated for several days.

Gingerbread

Bake this in a tinfoil pan and freeze it for an upcoming party.

2¼ cups flour
½ teaspoon baking soda
2 teaspoons ground ginger
1½ teaspoons cinnamon
¼ teaspoon ground cloves
½ teaspoon ground nutmeg
½ cup butter, softened
¾ cup molasses
¾ cup sugar
1 large egg
1 cup buttermilk
Whipped cream, for serving

Preheat the oven to 350°F. Spray an 11 x 8 x 2-inch baking pan with nonstick spray. In a medium bowl, combine the flour, baking soda, ginger, cinnamon, cloves, and nutmeg; set aside. In a large mixing bowl, beat the butter, molasses, sugar, and egg on medium speed until blended. Add the buttermilk on low speed until combined. Add the flour mixture and mix for about one minute. Pour the batter into the pan evenly. Bake for 40 - 45 minutes, or until the top springs back when lightly touched. Cool on a wire rack. Serve warm or at room temperature with whipped cream.

~Freeze~

When the cake is completely cooled, wrap in 2 layers of plastic wrap and 2 layers of heavy-duty aluminum foil. Freeze up to 1 month.

Granola Bars

Kids will enjoy making this snack for their lunch box.

3 cups quick cooking oatmeal

1 cup unsalted peanuts

1 cup raisins

1 cup sliced almonds

1½ teaspoons cinnamon

14 oz. sweetened condensed milk

½ cup butter, melted

¼ cup unsalted sunflower seeds

~A Day Ahead~

Preheat the oven to 325°F. Line a 15 x 10 x 1-inch sheet pan with aluminum foil and spray with nonstick spray. Stir all of the ingredients together in a large bowl. Pour onto the prepared pan. Spread out the mixture and press down to make it even. Bake for 25 - 30 minutes or until golden brown. Cool for 5 minutes in the pan. Then cut into bars. Place the bars on a wire rack to cool. Store loosely covered at room temperature.

Italian Cookies

(Shown on the back cover.) These cookies make a pretty gift around the holidays.

6 eggs
5 cups flour
2 cups confectioner's sugar
2½ tablespoons baking powder
1 cup shortening
4 teaspoons lemon extract
½ teaspoon almond extract

Glaze:
3¾ cups confectioner's sugar, sifted to remove the lumps
½ cup milk, warmed to room temperature
2 teaspoons vanilla extract
2 oz. colored sprinkles (nonpareils)

In a medium mixing bowl, beat the eggs on high speed until foamy, about 5 minutes; set aside. In a large mixing bowl, combine the flour, confectioner's sugar, and baking powder on low speed. Gradually add the shortening and extracts and beat until the dough resembles fine crumbs. Gradually add the beaten eggs. Prepare a large cookie sheet with parchment paper. Using a rounded tablespoon of dough, roll the dough into a ball and place on the prepared cookie sheet 2 inches apart. Bake at 350°F for 10 - 11 minutes. This is a dry cookie so do not overbake. Even if the cookie appears uncooked at 11 minutes, remove it from the oven. It will set up as it cools. Place the cookies on a wire rack.

To make the glaze, whisk the confectioner's sugar, milk, and extract in a small bowl until smooth. Dip the cookies in the glaze with a slotted spoon (coating them completely) and place the cookies on a wire rack. Immediately top with colored sprinkles or else the sprinkles won't stick. Makes 5 dozen.

~Freezing Directions for Uncooked Dough~

Shape the dough into balls using a rounded tablespoon of dough and place on a cookie sheet. Cover with plastic wrap. Freeze for 2 - 3 hours. Place the frozen dough balls in a labeled freezer bag. Write the cooking directions on the bag. Freeze up to 2 months.

~Thawing Out the Dough on Baking Day~

Cover a large cookie sheet with parchment paper and place the frozen cookie dough on the sheet pan about 2 inches apart. Thaw the cookie dough at room temperature for 30 - 45 minutes. Make the glaze (see directions above). Preheat the oven to 350°F and bake as directed.

Lemonade Cake

This is a great "make-ahead" dessert, as it tastes better the next day when the cake has absorbed all of the lemonade. The cake has great lemon flavor with a heavenly frosting that tastes like marshmallow.

1 box (18.25 oz.) lemon cake mix
6 oz. frozen lemonade concentrate (thawed)
¾ cup confectioner's sugar, sifted to remove the lumps

~A Day Ahead~

In a medium bowl, whisk the lemonade and confectioner's sugar together until smooth; set aside. Spray a 13 x 9 x 2-inch pan with nonstick spray. Prepare the cake mix as directed on the box and bake as directed. Cool the cake on a baking rack. (Do not remove the cake from the pan.) Poke holes in the warm cake every half inch using the handle-end of a spoon. Pour the lemonade mixture over the entire cake. When completely cool, cover with plastic wrap and refrigerate. Prepare the fluffy white frosting (below).

Fluffy White Frosting:

1 cup granulated sugar
⅓ cup water
¼ teaspoon cream of tartar
2 egg whites
1 teaspoon vanilla extract

In a small saucepan, mix the sugar, water, and cream of tartar. Cook and stir over medium-high heat until the sugar is dissolved and the mixture is clear and bubbly. Set aside to cool. In a medium mixing bowl, whip the egg whites and vanilla extract to soft peaks with the mixer. Continue whipping and slowly add the warm sugar mixture to the egg whites until stiff peaks form, about 4 - 7 minutes. Place the frosting in a covered container and refrigerate.

~Just before serving~

Spread the frosting over the cake evenly. Cover and store the cake in the refrigerator.

Lemon Lush

Lots of lemon flavor!

1 cup butter, softened
6 oz. cream cheese, softened
2 cups flour
8 oz. cream cheese, softened
1 cup confectioner's sugar, sifted to remove lumps
16 oz. whipped topping, divided
2 packages (3.4 oz. each) instant lemon pudding
2¾ cups whole milk

~A Day Ahead~

Preheat the oven to 350°F. In a large mixing bowl, beat the butter and 6 oz. of cream cheese until smooth. Add the flour and mix until thoroughly blended. Press the mixture evenly into the bottom of a 13 x 9 x 2-inch pan. (Dip your fingers in flour, so the mixture doesn't stick to your fingers when you press down.) Bake for about 38 minutes until lightly brown; set aside and cool. In a large mixing bowl, beat 8 oz. of cream cheese until smooth. Slowly add the confectioner's sugar to the cream cheese and beat until well blended. Fold in 2 cups of the whipped topping. Spread this mixture evenly over the cooled crust. Refrigerate for 30 minutes. In a medium bowl, whisk the pudding and milk together until thick, about 2 minutes. Spread the pudding evenly over the cream cheese mixture. Top with the remaining whipped topping. Cover and refrigerate until ready to serve.

Macadamia Nut Cookies

If you have a sweet tooth, you'll enjoy these big cookies!

2½ cups flour
1 teaspoon baking soda
½ teaspoon salt
1 cup butter, softened
¾ cup sugar
¾ cup light brown sugar, packed
1 large egg
1 teaspoon vanilla extract
1¼ cups macadamia nuts, chopped
1 cup vanilla chips

In a medium bowl, combine the flour, baking soda, and salt; set aside. In a large mixing bowl, cream the butter and sugars. Add the egg and vanilla and beat on medium speed until thoroughly combined. Add the flour mixture on low speed. Stir in the nuts and vanilla chips. Prepare a large sheet pan with parchment paper. For each cookie, shape ¼ cup of dough into a ball. Place the cookie dough 2 inches apart on the sheet pan and flatten the dough slightly with your fingers. Bake at 350°F for 13 minutes. Cool on a wire rack. Makes 20 large cookies

~Freezer Directions for Uncooked Dough~

Place the cookie dough balls on a large sheet pan in a single layer. Cover with plastic wrap. Freeze for 2 - 3 hours. Place the frozen cookie dough in labeled freezer bags and freeze up to 2 months. Be sure to write the cooking directions on the bag.

~Thawing Out the Dough on Baking Day~

Cover a large sheet pan with parchment paper and place the frozen cookie dough on it about 2 inches apart. Thaw the cookie dough at room temperature for 45 - 60 minutes. Preheat the oven to 350°F and bake for 13 minutes.

Maple Walnut Fudge

A great recipe for gifts, bake sales, and holiday fairs!

2 cups light brown sugar, packed
1 cup butter
⅔ cup evaporated milk
2 cups confectioner's sugar, sifted to remove lumps
1 teaspoon maple flavoring
1 cup walnuts, chopped

~Make Ahead~

Line an 8 x 8 x 2-inch baking pan with aluminum foil. Spray the foil lightly with nonstick spray. In a medium saucepan, combine the brown sugar, butter, and milk. Bring to a boil over medium heat. Stir constantly for 10 minutes. (Reduce the heat slightly if the mixture splatters your hand while stirring.) Remove the pan from the heat. Add the confectioner's sugar and maple flavoring. If you have a hand mixer, mix on medium speed for 3 minutes to remove the lumps. Otherwise, transfer the hot mixture to a medium mixing bowl and mix on medium speed until the lumps are removed. Fold in the walnuts and pour into the prepared pan. Refrigerate at least 4 hours. Pull up on the foil to remove the fudge from the pan. Peel the foil off of the fudge. Cut into squares. Cover and store at room temperature.

~Freeze~

Wrap the whole piece of fudge in plastic wrap and place in a labeled freezer bag. Freeze up to 2 months.

Be sure to thaw out the fudge completely before you cut it into squares.

Mini Cheesecakes

(Shown on the back cover.) This is a great "make-ahead" dessert, as it needs to set up overnight in the refrigerator.

1¼ cups graham crackers, crushed
¼ cup sugar
4 tablespoons butter, melted
2 (8 oz.) packages cream cheese, softened
2 large eggs
2 tablespoons fresh lemon juice
½ cup sugar
1 (21 oz.) can cherry or strawberry pie filling

~A Day Ahead~

Preheat the oven to 350°F. Line 18 regular muffin cups with paper baking cups. In a small bowl, mix the graham cracker crumbs, ¼ cup sugar, and melted butter. Place 2 tablespoons of the crumb mixture in each muffin cup. Press down on the crumbs with something flat to form a good crust. In a large mixing bowl, beat the cream cheese until fluffy. Add the eggs, lemon juice, and sugar and beat until smooth. Fill each baking cup with about 3 tablespoons of the cheesecake mixture. Bake the cheesecakes for 17 - 19 minutes or until they crack. Cool the cheesecakes in the muffin pan for 5 minutes, then remove them to a wire rack. Place the cooled cheesecakes (with the paper liners still on them) in a covered container and refrigerate overnight.

~Before Serving~

Remove the paper liners and top each cheesecake with 2 tablespoons of pie filling. Keep refrigerated. Makes 18 mini cheesecakes.

Oatmeal Cookies

A chewy, delicious classic!

2 cups old-fashioned oats
1 cup flour
1 teaspoon cinnamon
½ teaspoon ground nutmeg
1 teaspoon baking soda
½ teaspoon salt
12 tablespoons butter, softened
¾ cup light brown sugar, packed
½ cup sugar
1 large egg
1 teaspoon vanilla extract
¾ cup baking raisins
½ cup walnuts, chopped

Preheat the oven to 350°F. Line a large cookie sheet with parchment paper. In a medium bowl, combine the oats, flour, cinnamon, nutmeg, baking soda, and salt; set aside. In a large mixing bowl, cream the butter and sugars together until smooth. Beat in the egg and vanilla. Add the flour mixture to the creamed mixture and stir on low speed until combined. Stir in the raisins and walnuts. Shape the dough into balls using a rounded tablespoon of dough. Place the dough on the cookie sheet 2 inches apart. Bake for 12 minutes. The middles will be soft. Cool for 5 minutes on the baking sheet. Remove to a wire rack to cool.

~Freezing Directions for Uncooked Dough~

Place the cookie dough balls on a large sheet pan in a single layer. Cover with plastic wrap. Freeze for 3 hours. Place the dough in a labeled freezer bag and write the cooking directions on the bag. Freeze up to 2 months.

~Thawing Out the Dough on Baking Day~

Cover a large sheet pan with parchment paper. Place the cookie dough about 2 inches apart. Thaw the dough for 30 - 45 minutes. Preheat the oven to 350°F and bake for 12 - 14 minutes.

Peanut Butter Chocolate Chip Crackles

A great combination of peanut butter and chocolate!

½ cup shortening

¾ cup peanut butter

⅓ cup sugar

⅔ cup light brown sugar, packed

1 egg

2 tablespoons milk

1 teaspoon vanilla extract

1½ cups flour

1 teaspoon baking soda

½ teaspoon salt

1¼ cups semisweet chocolate chips

½ cup sugar (to coat the cookie)

Preheat the oven to 350°F. In a large mixing bowl, cream the shortening and peanut butter together. Add ⅓ cup of sugar, brown sugar, egg, milk, and vanilla; mix well. In a medium bowl, combine the flour, baking soda, and salt. Gradually add the dry mixture to the creamed mixture on low speed. Stir in the chocolate chips and mix well. Shape the dough into 1½-inch balls and roll in the sugar to coat. Prepare the cookie sheet with parchment paper and place the dough balls 2 inches apart on the sheet pan. Bake for 13 - 15 minutes. The cookie will be very soft in the middle. Do not overcook. It will set up as it cools. Cool for 5 minutes on the sheet pan, then transfer the cookies to a cooling rack. Makes 41 cookies.

~Freezing Directions for Uncooked Dough~

Shape the uncooked cookie dough into 1½-inch balls and roll in the sugar to coat. Place the cookie dough on a large enough cookie sheet to contain the dough in a single layer. Cover with plastic wrap and freeze for 2 - 3 hours. Place the frozen dough balls in a labeled freezer bag. Write the cooking directions on the bag. Freeze up to 2 months.

~Thawing Out the Dough on Baking Day~

Cover a large cookie sheet with parchment paper. Place the frozen cookie dough on top 2 inches apart. Thaw the cookie dough for 30 - 45 minutes. Preheat the oven to 350°F and bake the cookies for 13 - 15 minutes.

Peanut Butter Fudge

A great recipe for gifts, bake sales, and holiday fairs!

3 cups sugar
¾ cup milk
½ cup flour
1 cup peanut butter
1 cup Marshmallow Fluff
½ cup walnuts, chopped (optional)

~A Day Ahead~

Spray a 7 x 5 x 1½-inch baking dish with nonstick spray. In a 2 quart saucepan, stir the sugar and milk constantly over medium heat until it boils. Stir for 5 more minutes. Turn the heat off and keep the pan on the burner, as you quickly whisk in the flour, peanut butter, marshmallow, and walnuts. Pour the batter into the dish and smooth out the surface of the fudge with the back of a spoon quickly, as it sets up instantly. Cool the dish on a wire rack. Cut into squares when it is completely cooled. Cover and store at room temperature.

~Freeze~

Fudge freezes well if you freeze it whole. Wrap it in plastic wrap and place in a labeled freezer bag. Freeze up to 2 months. Be sure to thaw out the fudge completely before cutting it.

Peanut Butter Kiss Cookies

In my family, this is a must-have for the holidays!

9 oz. milk chocolate kisses
1½ cups flour
1 teaspoon baking soda
¼ teaspoon salt
⅛ teaspoon ground cinnamon
½ cup shortening
¾ cup peanut butter
⅓ cup sugar
⅓ cup light brown sugar, packed
1 large egg
2 tablespoons milk
1 teaspoon vanilla extract
⅓ cup sugar (to coat the cookie dough)

Remove the wrappers from 40 chocolate kisses and place them in a bowl. Preheat the oven to 350°F. In a medium bowl, combine the flour, baking soda, salt, and cinnamon; set aside. In a large mixing bowl, cream the shortening, peanut butter, ⅓ cup sugar and brown sugar. Add the egg, milk, and vanilla; beat well. Gradually add the dry ingredients to the creamed mixture on low speed. Prepare the cookie sheet with parchment paper. With a rounded tablespoon of dough, shape into balls and roll in ⅓ cup of sugar. Place on a cookie sheet 2 inches apart. Bake for 10 minutes. Do not overbake. This is a dry cookie and it will set up as it cools. Remove the cookie pan from the oven and press one chocolate kiss down on the center of each cookie. The cookie will crack and be very soft in the middle. Quickly use your fingers to push the soft cookie dough around the chocolate kiss so it doesn't move or fall off. Place the cookie sheet in the oven for 1 more minute to soften the chocolate. Remove the cookies and place on a wire rack to cool. Makes 40 cookies.

~Freezing Directions for Uncooked Dough~

Shape the dough into balls and roll in the sugar. Place the dough on a cookie sheet and cover with plastic wrap. Freeze for 2 - 3 hours. Place the frozen dough balls in a labeled freezer bag. Write the cooking directions on the bag. Freeze up to 2 months.

~Thawing Out the Dough on Baking Day~

Cover a large cookie sheet with parchment paper. Place the frozen cookie dough on the cookie sheet 2 inches apart. Thaw the cookie dough for 30 - 45 minutes. Preheat the oven to 350°F and follow the baking instructions.

Penuche Fudge

This is a great recipe for holiday fairs and gifts!

½ cup butter
1 cup light brown sugar, packed
¼ cup milk
3¾ cups confectioner's sugar, sifted to remove lumps
1 cup chopped walnuts

Line an 8 x 8 x 2-inch pan with aluminum foil. Spray the bottom and sides with nonstick spray; set aside. In a large saucepan, melt the butter on medium-low heat. Add the brown sugar; mix well. Stir constantly for 2 minutes. Increase the heat to medium. Stir in the milk and bring to a boil. Remove from heat. Cool the pan until you can comfortably rest your hand on the bottom of the pan and it feels warm. Beat in the confectioner's sugar until it's thick and a little hard to stir. Add the walnuts and mix well. Pour the fudge into the prepared pan. Pat down the fudge with the back of a spoon until the fudge is smooth and shiny on top. Refrigerate until firm. Cover and store at room temperature. Cut into squares.

~Freezing Directions~

This fudge freezes well if you freeze it whole. Prepare the fudge as directed. Cool it completely, cover it well in plastic wrap, and place it in a labeled freezer bag. Freeze up to 2 months. Be sure to thaw out the fudge completely before cutting it into squares.

Pound Cakes

A great dessert to keep in the freezer for an upcoming party!

2 tablespoons flour (to coat the pans)
3 cups flour
½ teaspoon baking powder
¼ teaspoon salt
2¾ cups sugar
1½ cups butter or margarine, softened
1½ teaspoons vanilla extract
6 large eggs
1 cup sour cream
Whipped cream
Frozen sweetened strawberries, thawed

Preheat the oven to 350°F. Spray two 9 x 5 x 3-inch loaf pans with nonstick spray and coat each pan with 1 tablespoon of flour. Tap out the excess flour. In a medium bowl, combine the flour, baking powder, and salt; set aside. In a large mixing bowl, cream the sugar and butter together until light and fluffy. On low speed, add the vanilla and each egg one at a time until well blended. Mix in the sour cream until blended and then add the flour mixture. Mix on medium speed for one minute. Pour the batter equally into both pans. Bake for 60 - 75 minutes. Test the cakes in the center with a toothpick during the last 15 minutes to check if they are done. The toothpick should come out clean or with a few moist crumbs attached. Cool the cakes on a wire rack. Serve with sweetened strawberries and whipped cream.

~Freeze~

When completely cooled, wrap the pound cake in plastic wrap and place it in a labeled freezer bag. Freeze up to 2 months.

Pumpkin Pie

This is a great Thanksgiving "make-ahead" dessert. Assemble this pie and freeze it (uncooked) a week or two before you need it. Then defrost it and bake it the day before Thanksgiving. It will save you time when you really need it.

15 oz. can pumpkin
14 oz. can sweetened condensed milk
2 large eggs
⅔ cup light brown sugar, packed
¼ cup sugar
1¼ teaspoons ground cinnamon
½ teaspoon ground ginger
½ teaspoon ground nutmeg
¼ teaspoon ground cloves
½ teaspoon salt
1 nine-inch frozen deep dish pie crust, thawed

~A Week or Two Ahead~

In a large mixing bowl, combine the first 10 ingredients and mix on medium speed for 2 minutes. Pour the mixture into the pie crust, filling it ¼ inch below the fluted edge. You will have extra batter left over. Place a sheet of wax paper over the pie, so that the pie mixture completely sticks to it for an air barrier. Trim the wax paper with scissors near the crust, so that it stays in place when you freeze it. Before you place the pie in an extra-large freezer bag, label the bag and write the following directions on it. Or write the directions on a piece of paper and place it in the bag with the pie. Freeze up to 2 months.

Directions:

Thaw the pie in the refrigerator for 8 hours. Preheat the oven to 425°F. Remove the wax paper carefully and place the pie on a large sheet pan. Bake at 425°F for 15 minutes. Reduce the heat to 350°F and bake for 50 minutes. Cool completely on a wire rack. Cover and refrigerate.

Snickerdoodle Cookies

A soft, delicious cookie for all ages!

2¾ cups flour
1¼ teaspoons baking soda
2 teaspoons cream of tartar
¼ teaspoon salt
½ cup butter
½ cup shortening
1½ cups cups sugar
2 large eggs
2 tablespoons sugar
2 teaspoons cinnamon

Preheat the oven to 350°F. Prepare a large sheet pan with parchment paper; set aside. In a medium bowl, mix the flour, baking soda, cream of tartar, and salt; set aside. In a medium mixing bowl, cream the butter, shortening, and 1½ cups sugar. Blend in the eggs on low speed. Add the flour mixture and mix until combined. In a very small bowl, combine the sugar and cinnamon. Roll 1 tablespoon of cookie dough into a ball and roll in the cinnamon mixture. Place the cookie dough on the sheet pan 2 inches apart. Bake at 350°F for 8 - 9 minutes. Do not overbake. The centers will be soft but will set upon cooling. Cool on a wire rack. Makes 4½ dozen cookies.

~Freezing Directions for Uncooked Dough~

Place the sugar coated cookie dough on a large sheet pan in a single layer. Cover with plastic wrap and freeze for 2 - 3 hours. Place the dough in a labeled freezer bag. Write the cooking directions on the bag. Freeze up to 2 months.

~Thawing Out the Dough on Baking Day~

Cover a large sheet pan with parchment paper and place the frozen dough 2 inches apart. Thaw the dough for 30 - 45 minutes. Preheat the oven to 350°F and bake for 8 - 10 minutes.

Tiramisu

This is the perfect "make-ahead" dessert, as it needs a whole day to set up properly before serving. It has become one of our favorite desserts.

1¼ cups strong brewed coffee
¾ teaspoon instant espresso coffee
1 tablespoon brandy
6 large egg yolks
⅔ cup sugar
3 tablespoons brandy
3 cups mascarpone cheese
¾ cup heavy cream
3 oz. package soft lady fingers (found in the bakery section)
1½ tablespoons Dutch-processed cocoa

Combine the coffee, espresso, and 1 tablespoon of brandy in a shallow bowl; set aside to cool. In a large mixing bowl, beat the egg yolks and sugar on medium speed for 2 minutes. Add 3 tablespoons of brandy and the mascarpone cheese. Beat on medium speed until smooth about 1 - 2 minutes; set aside. In a medium mixing bowl, add the cream and slowly increase the speed to high. Whip for 1½ to 2 minutes until stiff peaks can be formed. Add the whipped cream to the mascarpone mixture and fold in gently; set aside. Dip the lady fingers quickly into the coffee, one at a time, lightly coating both sides. (You don't want them completely soggy.) Place them in an 8 x 12 x 2-inch baking dish, making one layer of them in the bottom of the dish. Spread the mascarpone mixture over the lady fingers evenly. Cover and refrigerate overnight. (It needs a day to set up properly.) Just before serving, sift the cocoa over the Tiramisu, covering it completely.

Walnut Tassies

This is a great dessert to bring to a baby or bridal shower, as they are little bite-size treats.

Crust:

1 cup butter, softened

6 oz. cream cheese, softened

2 cups flour

Filling:

1 egg

¾ cup light brown sugar, packed

1 tablespoon butter, melted

¾ cup walnuts, finely chopped

⅛ teaspoon salt

Preheat the oven to 350°F. In a large mixing bowl, beat the butter and cream cheese on medium speed until smooth. Add the flour on low speed and mix until thoroughly combined. Divide the dough into about 30 balls, using 1 tablespoon of dough for each ball. Press each ball of dough into an ungreased mini muffin cup to form a mini pie crust. Keep the top of the crust no higher than the rim of each muffin cup. Set the muffin tins aside.

In a medium mixing bowl, mix the egg, brown sugar, butter, walnuts, and salt, until combined. Add the filling to each crust, filling it no more than half full. Bake at 350°F for 20 minutes. Reduce the heat to 250°F and bake about 14 minutes longer. Remove the walnut tassies to a wire rack to cool. Makes 30 walnut tassies.

~Freeze~

When the walnut tassies are completely cool, place them in labeled freezer bags in a single layer. Freeze up to 3 months.

Main Dishes

Baked Chicken Chimichangas
Baked Manicotti
BBQ Country Ribs/Pulled Pork
BBQ Pepper Jack Chicken
Broiled Honey Mustard Salmon
Cheesy Pasta, Ham, and Peas
Chicken and Spinach Stuffed Shells
Chicken Cannelloni
Chicken Cordon Bleu
Chicken Enchiladas
Chicken Marsala with a Twist
Chicken Meatballs/Burgers
Chicken Parmesan
Chicken Piccata
Chicken Stroganoff
Chicken Tortellini Tetrazzini
Crab Cakes
Haddock with Ritz Topping
Honey Mustard Chicken Fingers
Italian Restaurant Chicken
Lasagna
London Broil Strips
Marinated Steak

Meatballs and Gravy in the Crock-Pot
Meat Pies
Mini Meatloaves
Mushroom Burgers
Panko Breaded Pork Medallions
Pork Florentine
Prosciutto Wrapped Stuffed Chicken
Sausage Calzones
Sausage Quesadillas
Shepherd's Pie
Sloppy Joes
Spaghetti Sauce
Steak Fajitas
Stuffed Beef Tenderloin
Stuffed Cornish Hens
Taco Lasagna
Taco Pie
Tacos
Teriyaki Chicken
Thai Chicken Thighs
Tuna Noodle Casserole
Turkey Burgers

Baked Chicken Chimichangas

For a quick meal, cook the chicken mixture a day ahead or freeze it for another time.

3 tablespoons olive oil, divided
1½ lbs. chicken breast, cut into bite-size pieces
½ teaspoon salt
½ teaspoon ground black pepper
½ cup onions, diced
½ cup green bell pepper, diced
1 teaspoon ground cumin
½ teaspoon cayenne red pepper
½ teaspoon dried oregano
½ cup thick and chunky salsa (mild or medium)
8 (8 inch) flour tortillas
2 cups four cheese Mexican shredded cheese

~Cooking Directions~

In a large skillet with 2 tablespoons of olive oil, brown the chicken on medium-high heat until no longer pink. Season the chicken with salt and pepper. Place the cooked chicken in a bowl. Reduce the heat to medium and add 1 tablespoon of olive oil to the skillet. Sauté the onion, green pepper, cumin, cayenne pepper, and oregano until tender. Add the chicken back to the pan and cook until heated through, stirring often. Stir in the salsa and heat for one minute. Set the pan aside. Preheat the oven to 400°F. Spray a large sheet pan with nonstick spray; set aside. Heat the stack of tortillas between 2 damp paper towels in the microwave for 20 - 40 seconds on high to make them easier to bend. For each chimichanga, place ½ cup of the chicken mixture in the center of the tortilla. Sprinkle ¼ cup of the cheese on top. Fold in the opposite sides of the tortilla over the chicken mixture. Roll up the tortilla, enclosing the mixture, and place it seam-side down on the sheet pan. Make the rest of the chimichangas and place them on the sheet pan. Spray the tops of the chimichangas with nonstick spray. Bake 10 minutes. Serve with sour cream.

~Freeze~

Cover and refrigerate the chicken mixture. When completely cooled, place the chicken mixture in a labeled freezer bag. The flour tortillas can be frozen separately. Keep frozen up to 3 months.

Baked Manicotti

This recipe makes about 16 stuffed manicotti. Prepare one pan for dinner and freeze another pan for another meal.

32 oz. part-skim ricotta cheese
2 cups grated Parmesan cheese, divided
3½ cups shredded mozzarella cheese, divided
2 large eggs
½ teaspoon salt
½ teaspoon ground black pepper
¼ cup fresh parsley, chopped
2 boxes (8 oz. each) manicotti
5½ cups spaghetti sauce

~A Day Ahead~

In a large bowl, combine the ricotta, 1½ cups Parmesan cheese, 1½ cups mozzarella cheese, eggs, salt, pepper, and parsley; set aside. Boil 20 manicotti, just in case they fall apart. Cook them 1 minute less than directed on the box. Do not overcook, as the pasta will split and fall apart. When the manicotti are done cooking, remove them with a slotted spoon and carefully place them on a sheet of waxed paper in a single layer to air dry. Coat the bottom of two 11 x 9 x 2-inch baking pans with sauce. Fill a pastry bag with the ricotta mixture and fill each manicotti. Place 8 manicotti in a single layer in each pan. Top with desired amount of spaghetti sauce. Sprinkle ¼ cup of Parmesan cheese over the top of each pan. Sprinkle 1 cup of mozzarella cheese over each pan. Cover and refrigerate, or freeze the pans wrapped in plastic wrap and 2 layers of foil when completely cooled. It can be frozen up to 2 months.

~Cooking Directions~

Remove the manicotti pan from the refrigerator 30 minutes before baking. Bake the manicotti, covered, at 350°F for about 30 minutes. Uncover and bake until bubbly about 15 minutes.

If frozen, thaw it out in the refrigerator for about 24 hours. Be sure to remove the manicotti from the refrigerator 30 minutes before baking. Bake as directed above.

BBQ Country Ribs / Pulled Pork

If your family doesn't eat all of the meat when you make the BBQ Country Ribs, keep the leftover sauce and meat for pulled pork sandwiches.

4 lbs. country-style pork ribs
1½ cups barbecue sauce
¼ cup light brown sugar, packed
¼ cup apricot jam
¼ cup pineapple jam
⅛ teaspoon red pepper flakes
2 tablespoons tapioca
Hamburger buns (for pulled pork sandwiches)

~BBQ Country Ribs~

Heat a large slow cooker on low heat. Place the pork in the slow cooker. Mix the rest of the ingredients in a medium bowl. Pour the sauce over the pork and mix well. Cook 5 - 6 hours until fork tender. Serves 5.

~Pulled Pork Sandwiches~

When the pork is cooked, remove the bones and shred the pork with 2 forks. Return the meat to the sauce. Use a large slotted spoon to scoop the meat onto a hamburger bun or sub roll.

~Freeze~

Freeze desired portions of pulled pork/sauce in labeled containers for sandwiches.

BBQ Pepper Jack Chicken

With a little prep work the night before, you can make this in no time for a weeknight meal.

4 boneless, skinless chicken breasts
1¼ cup freshly shredded Pepper Jack cheese
4 – 6 slices bacon, cut into ½-inch pieces
1 tablespoon olive oil
Salt and black ground pepper
4 tablespoons barbecue sauce

~A Day Ahead~

Clean and pound the chicken to ½-inch thickness. Place the chicken in a sealed bag and refrigerate. Shred the cheese, place in a covered container and refrigerate. Cook the bacon until browned. Drain and cool the bacon on paper towels. Place the bacon in a covered bowl and refrigerate.

~Cooking Directions~

Preheat the oven to 400°F. Heat the oil in a large nonstick skillet over medium-high heat. Season the chicken with salt and pepper. Brown the chicken on both sides. Place the chicken on a sheet pan. Spread 1 tablespoon of barbecue sauce on each piece of chicken. Sprinkle the cheese evenly over the 4 pieces of chicken. Sprinkle the bacon pieces over the top. Bake the chicken for 10 - 12 minutes. Serves 4.

Broiled Honey Mustard Salmon

Fresh fish should be cooked the day you buy it, so get to the fish market early in the day, and let this marinate in the refrigerator until dinnertime. It's delicious, healthy, and quick!

4 salmon fillets (½ lb. each)
¼ cup honey
¼ cup spicy brown mustard
1 teaspoon dried dill weed

~Up to 8 Hours Ahead~

Rinse the fish under cold water and pat dry with paper towels. Place the fish in a baking dish. In a small bowl, mix the honey, mustard, and dill. Pour it over the fish. Turn the fish coating both sides. Cover with plastic wrap and refrigerate.

~Cooking Directions~

Take the fish out of the refrigerator 30 minutes before cooking. Set the oven rack to the upper middle level. Preheat the broiler. Broil the fish for about 5 minutes on the first side. Flip the fish over when the top half of the fish looks cooked. Broil for 5 - 7 minutes on the other side. When the fish flakes easily with a fork, it is done. Do not overcook. Serves 4.

Cheesy Pasta, Ham, and Peas

This is a delicious recipe to use up your leftover spiral ham!

4 cups casserole or large elbow pasta, uncooked
5 cups whole milk
½ cup butter
½ cup flour
½ cup Cheez Whiz Original Cheese Dip
½ teaspoon salt
½ teaspoon black ground pepper
4 cups ham, cubed
1½ cups frozen petite peas

~A Day Ahead~

Spray a 13 x 9 x 2-inch baking dish with nonstick spray; set aside. Cook the elbows according to the directions on the box; drain and set aside. Warm the milk in the microwave for about 2 minutes on high; set aside. In a large skillet, melt the butter over medium-low heat. Add the flour and whisk for one minute. Slowly add the milk and whisk constantly. Turn the heat up to medium and stir until thickened. Remove the pan from the heat. Add the Cheez Whiz and stir until melted. Season the sauce with salt and pepper. Stir in the ham, peas, and cooked elbows; mix well. Transfer to the baking dish and spread evenly. Allow it to cool before covering it with foil. Refrigerate until time to reheat.

~Cooking Directions~

Take the dish out of the refrigerator 30 minutes before cooking. Preheat the oven to 350°F. Cover and bake for 30 - 45 minutes or until bubbly. Serves 8 - 9.

Chicken and Spinach Stuffed Shells

This recipe stuffs 20 jumbo shells. Cook extra shells in case they rip apart when cooking. If you are freezing this recipe, I would suggest freezing the stuffed shells in two 8 x 8 x 2-inch foil pans. If you use foil pans, you won't have to worry about getting your pans back, if you bring this to a potluck dinner.

6 oz. baby spinach
1 cup water
12 oz. box jumbo shells
15 oz. ricotta cheese, part skim
1 large egg
½ cup Parmesan cheese, grated
1 rotisserie chicken, cooked, all meat removed and shredded
½ cup mozzarella cheese, shredded
½ teaspoon salt
¼ teaspoon black ground pepper
3 - 4 cups spaghetti sauce
8 oz. shredded Italian cheese blend

~A Day Ahead~

In a medium saucepan, boil the spinach with 1 cup of water until wilted. Drain and chop the spinach; set aside. Cook the shells as directed on the package. Drain the shells and place them on a long piece of wax paper to dry. In a large bowl, combine the ricotta, egg, Parmesan cheese, chicken, spinach, mozzarella cheese, salt, and pepper. Coat the bottom of two 8 x 8 x 2-inch pans with sauce. Stuff the shells with the chicken mixture and place them in the pan facing up. Sprinkle all of the stuffed shells with Italian cheese. Cover both pans with foil and place in the refrigerator until you are ready to cook them.

~Cooking Directions~

Remove the pans from the refrigerator 30 minutes before baking. Preheat the oven to 350°F. Cover and bake for 30 minutes. Uncover and bake 20 - 25 minutes until bubbly.

~Freeze~

Wrap the uncooked stuffed shells (with sauce and cheese) in plastic wrap and 2 layers of foil. Label with cooking directions and freeze up to 3 months. Be sure to thaw the pans in the refrigerator at least 24 hours in advance before cooking.

Chicken Cannelloni

(Shown on the back cover.) Okay, I know what you're thinking. This is too many ingredients! It'll take all day! That's the beauty of make-ahead meals. You can assemble all of this the day before you cook it. This is a great dish for a dinner party or a buffet.

1½ lbs. boneless, skinless chicken breast, cooked and shredded
10 oz. bag spinach, cooked, drained, and chopped
15 oz. ricotta cheese, part skim
½ cup mozzarella cheese, shredded
½ teaspoon salt
½ teaspoon black ground pepper
3 garlic cloves, minced
½ cup Parmesan cheese, grated
2 eggs
8 oz. box manicotti

Sauce:
3 cups heavy cream
½ teaspoon chicken bouillon powder
1 large garlic clove, minced
1 cup 4-cheese pizza cheese, shredded
Salt and pepper, to taste
Additional Parmesan cheese, for the topping

~A Day Ahead~

Spray a 13 x 9 x 2-inch baking dish with nonstick spray; set aside. In a large bowl, combine the shredded chicken, spinach, ricotta, mozzarella, salt, pepper, garlic,

Parmesan cheese, and eggs. Boil the manicotti 1 minute less than directed on the box. Do not overcook. You will need 12 manicotti, but it is good to cook extra in case they fall apart. (There are 14 manicotti per box.) Carefully remove the manicotti from the hot water and place them on a long sheet of wax paper to cool and dry. Fill a pastry bag with the chicken mixture and stuff the manicotti. Place the stuffed manicotti (side by side and touching) in the baking dish. Or you can divide them up into 2 freezable baking pans. To make the sauce: Heat a large skillet over medium heat. Add the cream. When the cream is hot, stir in the bouillon, garlic, shredded cheese, and salt and pepper to taste. Stir until well blended. Pour the sauce over the cannelloni. Cover and refrigerate.

~Cooking Directions~

Take the cannelloni out of the refrigerator 30 minutes before cooking. Preheat the oven to 350°F. Sprinkle the top of the cannelloni with Parmesan cheese. Cover and bake for 30 minutes. Then uncover and bake 20 - 25 minutes until bubbly and the cheese on top is golden brown. Serves 6 (2 manicotti each).

~Freezing Directions~

This dish will taste just fine after it has been frozen, but be aware that the cream will separate. If you want to freeze the cannelloni, be sure that it is completely cooled first. Then wrap it well in plastic wrap and place it in a labeled extra-large freezer bag or 2 layers of foil. On the outside of the bag, write "Sprinkle with grated Parmesan cheese before cooking." This will freeze up to 2 months.

~Thawing Directions~

Transfer the frozen cannelloni dish to the refrigerator at least 24 hours before you want to cook it. Remove it from the refrigerator 30 minutes before cooking. Cook as directed. You may have to add on a little cooking time, if it's not completely thawed out.

Chicken Cordon Bleu

Double the recipe for a nice dinner party. It's not a lot of work if you prepare the chicken a day ahead.

4 skinless, boneless chicken breasts
4 thin slices Swiss cheese
4 thin slices Virginia baked ham
½ cup flour
2 teaspoons paprika
1 teaspoon salt
½ teaspoon white or black pepper
6 tablespoons butter
½ cup dry white wine (Pinot Grigio)
1 teaspoon chicken bouillon powder
1 cup light cream
2 tablespoons cornstarch
Salt and pepper, to taste

~A Day Ahead~

Rinse and dry the chicken with paper towels. Pound the chicken, so that each piece is ½-inch thick. Place a slice of cheese and ham on each breast. Roll them up and secure with 2 toothpicks. The toothpicks will hold better, if you cross them like an "X." Place the rolled up chicken on a dish, cover, and refrigerate. Combine the flour, paprika, salt, and pepper in a shallow dish. Cover it and leave on the counter, until you are ready to cook the chicken.

~Cooking Directions~

Remove the chicken from the refrigerator 30 minutes before cooking. Roll the chicken in the flour mixture and set aside. Heat the butter in a large nonstick skillet over medium heat. Brown the chicken on all sides. Place the chicken on a plate. Add the wine and bouillon to the pan and stir until the bouillon is dissolved and blended. Reduce the heat to medium-low. Add the chicken back to the pan. Cover the chicken and simmer for 30 minutes, or until the juices run clear. Remove the chicken to a plate. Increase the heat to medium. Add the cream and whisk in the cornstarch. Stir until it thickens. Season the sauce with salt and pepper. Turn the heat down to low and add the chicken back to the skillet. Coat the chicken with the sauce, cover the pan, and heat the chicken for 15 minutes. Coat the chicken with the sauce when serving.

Chicken Enchiladas

If you like Mexican food, this is worth the effort!

28 oz. can tomatillos
1 quart low-sodium chicken broth
4 jalapeno peppers, finely diced
1 shallot, minced
1 teaspoon dried oregano
3 cloves garlic, minced
½ teaspoon salt
½ teaspoon ground black pepper
3 tablespoons flour
4 tablespoons water
2 lbs. boneless, skinless chicken breasts
Salt and pepper, to taste
1 tablespoon canola oil
3 cups low-sodium chicken broth
4 cups shredded Mexican 4 cheese, divided
20 small corn tortillas

~A Day Ahead~

Drain the tomatillos and puree them in a food processor or blender. In a large saucepan, add the pureed tomatillos, 1 quart of chicken broth, jalapenos, shallot, oregano, garlic, salt and pepper. Bring to a boil over high heat, cover and reduce the heat to medium and cook for 15 minutes. In a small bowl, whisk 3 tablespoons of flour with 4 tablespoons of water until smooth. Add the flour mixture to the tomatillo sauce. Whisk until thickened, about 5 minutes. Set aside to cool.

Rinse the chicken under cool water and pat dry with paper towels. Season the chicken with salt and pepper. In a large Dutch oven over medium-high heat, add the oil and brown the chicken on both sides. Add 3 cups of chicken broth and bring to a boil on high heat. Reduce to medium-low and simmer for 20 minutes, or until the chicken is cooked through. Remove the chicken and place on a plate to cool. When cool enough to handle, shred the chicken with a fork and place the chicken in a large mixing bowl. Add 2 cups of the tomatillo sauce and 2 cups of the cheese to the chicken. Mix together until well combined. In a 13 x 9 x 2-inch baking dish, pour enough of the sauce to coat the bottom of the dish; set aside. Place 10 tortillas between two damp paper towels on a microwavable plate. Heat the tortillas in the microwave for one minute on 100% power. (This will make them more pliable without cracking.) Take one tortilla at a time and place ¼ cup of chicken mixture across the center. Roll up tightly and place seam-side down in the baking dish. You will want to place them close together, so you can fit a good amount. This size dish will hold about 10 enchiladas. Pour 1 cup of the sauce evenly over all of the enchiladas. Sprinkle 1 cup of cheese evenly over the top. Cover with plastic wrap and refrigerate until ready to cook or wrap well and freeze. It is best to bake this within 24 hours, as it will get soggy.

You should have enough to make about 6 more enchiladas in a smaller 8 x 8 x 2-inch pan to cook or freeze.

~Cooking Directions~

Remove the enchiladas from the refrigerator 30 minutes before baking. Preheat the oven to 350°F. Cover and bake for 30 - 35 minutes. Uncover and cook for 10 - 15 minutes. I like to serve this with sour cream and Mexican rice. The whole recipe will serve 6 - 8 people.

Chicken Marsala with a Twist

The prosciutto and melted Fontina cheese really make this a special dish! It is important that you use fine Marsala wine from the liquor store. It makes a big difference.

1 tablespoon olive oil
4 chicken breasts, pounded ½-inch thin
½ teaspoon salt
½ teaspoon ground black pepper
6 tablespoons butter
1 shallot, minced
3 large cloves garlic, minced
1½ cups mushrooms, sliced
¼ teaspoon salt
¼ teaspoon black ground pepper
½ cup fine Marsala wine
⅓ cup fresh basil, chopped
1 tablespoon fresh lemon juice
1 to 2 tablespoons butter
4 thin slices of prosciutto ham
½ - ¾ cup Fontina cheese, shredded

~A Day Ahead~

Heat the olive oil in a large skillet over medium-high heat. Season the chicken with salt and pepper. Sauté the chicken on both sides until lightly browned. Remove the chicken to a plate; keep covered. Take the pan off of the heat for a few minutes to cool down a bit. Reduce the heat to medium and add the butter to the skillet. Sauté the shallot, garlic, and mushrooms until tender, about 3 minutes. Season with salt and pepper. Add the wine, basil, and lemon juice. Stir for about 2 minutes. Stir in 1 to 2 tablespoons of butter. Return the chicken to the skillet; coat with sauce. Cover and cook for 5 minutes. Place 1 slice of prosciutto on top of each chicken breast. Sprinkle the cheese on top of the prosciutto. Cover the pan until the cheese is melted about 3 minutes. Transfer the chicken and sauce to a baking dish. Cool and cover with plastic wrap. Refrigerate until ready to reheat. Serves 4.

~Heating Directions~

This reheats very nicely in the microwave.

Chicken Meatballs/Burgers

Cook and freeze the meatballs for a spaghetti dinner or for quick meatball subs.

1 lb. ground chicken
1 egg
½ cup Parmesan cheese, grated
½ cup seasoned bread crumbs
2 garlic cloves, minced
2 tablespoons chopped fresh basil
½ teaspoon salt
¼ teaspoon ground black pepper

Preheat the oven to 350°F. Combine all of the ingredients in a large bowl. Shape into 1-inch meatballs and place them on a broiler pan. Bake for 25 minutes. Cool the meatballs on a clean large sheet pan. When they are completely cool, wrap the sheet pan with plastic wrap and freeze for 2 - 3 hours. Place the meatballs in a labeled freezer bag and freeze up to 3 months.

~Variations~

Chicken Burgers

Divide the chicken mixture evenly into 4 burgers. Broil or grill about 10 minutes on each side. Serve on a toasted hamburger bun with any of the following: cheese, lettuce, tomatoes, or pickles. Or freeze the chicken burgers (uncooked) for a later time.

Chicken Parmesan Burgers

Grill or broil the burgers. Top with a bit of spaghetti sauce and melt some mozzarella cheese on top. Place on toasted hamburger buns.

Chicken Parmesan

In my opinion, nothing beats fresh bread crumbs for this recipe. When you have the time, buy a fresh loaf of French bread and grate it in the food processor. Freeze 3 cups of the bread crumbs in a labeled freezer bag. Freeze the rest of the bread crumbs for other recipes. This will cut down on your prep time when you want to make this. Just thaw out the bread crumbs for 30 minutes before you need them.

5 chicken breasts, pounded ¼- to ½-inch thin
½ cup freshly grated Parmesan cheese (Parmigiano Reggiano)
3 cups freshly grated bread crumbs
½ teaspoon dried oregano
½ teaspoon salt
½ teaspoon black ground pepper
2 egg whites
¼ cup water
2 tablespoons olive oil
2 tablespoons butter
1¼ cups spaghetti sauce
12 oz. package fresh mozzarella cheese (sliced into ten ¼-inch slices)

~A Day Ahead~

Clean the chicken breasts and pat them dry with paper towels. Place them between plastic wrap and pound them thin, so they are all uniform in size. Place them in a sealed bag and refrigerate. Grate the cheese and place it in a sealed bag with the bread crumbs, oregano, salt, and pepper. Refrigerate the bread crumb mixture.

~Cooking Directions~

Preheat the oven to 400°F. Spray a large sheet pan with nonstick spray; set aside. Place the bread crumb mixture in a shallow bowl; set aside. Beat the egg whites and water in a separate shallow bowl; set aside. Heat the olive oil and butter in a large nonstick skillet over medium heat. Coat the chicken with egg whites. Then roll the chicken in the bread crumbs (coating them heavily). Brown the chicken on both sides in two or three batches if necessary. Turn the heat down if the oil/butter browns too much. Add more olive oil/butter if needed. Place the browned chicken on the sheet pan. Spread the spaghetti sauce evenly over each piece of chicken. Place 2 slices of cheese on each piece. Bake for 10 - 15 minutes. Serves 5.

Chicken Piccata

This is a great dish for a potluck dinner, as it feeds a lot of people.

1 cup flour
½ teaspoon salt
½ teaspoon black ground pepper
3 lbs. chicken breast, cut into 2-inch strips
4 tablespoons olive oil
4 tablespoons butter
5 cloves garlic, minced
2 tablespoons flour
⅔ cup white wine (Pinot Grigio)
⅔ cup low sodium chicken broth
5 tablespoons fresh lemon juice

~A Day Ahead~

In a shallow bowl, combine 1 cup of flour with salt and pepper. Coat the chicken pieces in the flour and set aside. Heat the oil in a large nonstick skillet over medium heat. Brown the chicken on both sides until lightly brown. (You may need to do this in 2 or 3 batches.) Place the cooked chicken in a 12 x 8 x 2-inch baking dish. Carefully remove any oil in the skillet with paper towels. Cool the pan down a bit off the burner. Return the skillet to medium heat. Melt the butter and add the garlic. Stir constantly for 30 seconds. Add 2 tablespoons of flour to the pan. Stir for 1 minute. Add the wine, broth, and lemon juice; mix well. Pour the sauce over the chicken and stir until all the chicken is well coated. Cool, cover, and refrigerate.

~Cooking Directions~

Remove the baking dish from the refrigerator 30 minutes before cooking. Preheat the oven to 400°F. Stir the chicken, cover the dish with foil, and bake for 20 – 24 minutes until heated through. Serves 7.

Chicken Stroganoff

If you're looking for good old comfort food, this recipe is for you!

1¾ lbs. boneless, skinless chicken breasts
12 oz. mushrooms
¼ cup onion, diced
3 tablespoons canola oil
2 tablespoons flour
1½ cups low sodium chicken broth
1½ cups low sodium beef broth
3½ cups wide pasta noodles
⅓ cup sour cream
Salt and pepper, to taste

~A Day Ahead~

Rinse the chicken and pat them dry. Cut the chicken into 1½-inch strips (about ¼-inch thick). Place the chicken in a sealed bag and refrigerate. Clean the mushrooms with a paper towel and discard the stems. Slice the mushrooms, place them in a bag, and refrigerate. Place the diced onion in a container and refrigerate.

~Cooking Directions~

Heat the oil in a large skillet over medium-high heat. Add the chicken to the skillet and season with salt and pepper. Stir occasionally until no longer pink. Remove the chicken to a bowl. Add the mushrooms and onion to the skillet. Season lightly with salt. Add more oil if it is too dry. Stir occasionally for 5 minutes. Add the flour and stir constantly for less than a minute. Stir in the broth and add the chicken back to the pan. Bring to a simmer. Then turn the heat down to low. Stir in the noodles and cover for about 12 minutes, stirring occasionally. Remove the pan from the heat and stir in the sour cream. Serve immediately. Serves 5.

Chicken Tortellini Tetrazzini

With a little help from a store-bought, cooked, rotisserie chicken, this recipe comes together in no time!

20 oz. herb chicken tortellini
¼ cup butter
1 to 2 cloves garlic, minced
¼ cup flour
1 cup chicken broth
1 cup light cream
½ teaspoon salt
½ teaspoon black ground pepper
1 rotisserie chicken, cooked, all meat removed and shredded
1½ cups frozen petite peas
1 cup Parmesan cheese, grated
Salt & pepper, to taste
Additional freshly grated Parmesan cheese for serving

~A Day Ahead~

Cook the tortellini one minute less than directed on the package. Drain the pasta and set aside. In a large skillet, melt the butter over medium-low heat. Add the garlic and stir for 30 seconds. Add the flour and whisk for 1 minute. Turn the heat up to medium. Stir in the chicken broth and cream. Season with salt and pepper. Bring to a boil and add the chicken, peas, and tortellini. (You can add more chicken broth if you think it is too dry.) Add the Parmesan cheese and mix well. Season lightly with salt and pepper. Pour into a 13 x 9 x 2-inch baking dish. Cool, cover, and refrigerate.

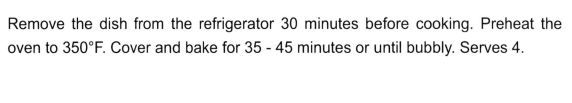

~Cooking Directions~

Remove the dish from the refrigerator 30 minutes before cooking. Preheat the oven to 350°F. Cover and bake for 35 - 45 minutes or until bubbly. Serves 4.

Crab Cakes

You can make crab cake sandwiches or eat them as an appetizer.

18 oz. fresh lump crab meat, drained
⅓ cup mayonnaise
1 large egg
½ teaspoon Worcestershire sauce
¼ teaspoon celery salt
¼ teaspoon paprika
¼ teaspoon sea salt
¼ teaspoon ground black pepper
2 tablespoons fresh parsley, chopped
2 tablespoons scallions, thinly sliced
¼ cup Saltine crackers, crushed
2 teaspoons olive oil

In a large bowl, mix the mayonnaise, egg, Worcestershire sauce, celery salt, paprika, salt, pepper, parsley, scallions, and cracker crumbs. Mix in the crabmeat gently. Use ½ cup of the crab mixture to form a flat, round crab cake. Do not make it too thick. Cover the crab cakes and refrigerate up to 8 hours. Heat the olive oil in a nonstick skillet over medium heat. Brown the crab cakes for 5 - 6 minutes on each side. I enjoy these on a hamburger bun. Makes 5 crab cakes.

If you'd like to freeze the crab cakes uncooked, wrap them individually with plastic wrap and place them in a labeled freezer bag. Freeze up to 3 months. When you are ready to cook them, defrost them completely in the microwave first. Cook as directed.

Haddock with Ritz Topping

This is a quick recipe. But if you want to make part of it ahead, you can crush the crackers and place them in a sealed bag with the salt and pepper. You can also place the measured butter in a microwavable bowl, cover it, and store it in the refrigerator. This will help get dinner on the table that much faster.

2 lbs. fresh haddock, skinned
2½ cups crushed Ritz crackers
½ teaspoon salt
½ teaspoon ground black pepper
¾ cup butter, melted

Preheat the oven to 350°F. Rinse and dry the fish with paper towels. Place the fish in a baking dish (in one layer). Mix the crackers, salt, and pepper with the melted butter. Sprinkle evenly over the fish. Bake uncovered for 20 minutes. Then broil on the middle rack for 4 - 5 minutes. Serve with tartar sauce.

Note: Plan on ½ lb. of fish for each person.

Honey Mustard Chicken Fingers

An easy recipe for the kids!

6 tablespoons spicy brown mustard
2 tablespoons honey
1½ lbs. chicken tenders
1½ cups plain bread crumbs

~A Day Ahead~

In a gallon-size storage bag, combine the mustard and honey. Rinse and dry the chicken tenders and place them in the bag. Seal the bag well and turn the bag several times to coat the chicken. Refrigerate until you are ready to cook. Place the measured bread crumbs in a shallow container, cover it, and leave it on the counter.

~Cooking Directions~

Preheat the oven to 425°F. Spray a 15 x 10 x 1-inch sheet pan with nonstick spray. Coat each chicken tender with the bread crumbs and place on the baking sheet. Spray the tops of the chicken with nonstick spray. Bake for 20 - 25 minutes until browned and cooked through. Serves 4.

Italian Restaurant Chicken

(Shown on the cover.) This is the kind of dish you would find in an Italian restaurant. I highly recommend using Parmigiano-Reggiano cheese in this recipe. It makes a huge difference!

1¾ lbs. fresh chicken tenders
Salt and pepper (to season the chicken)
1 teaspoon Italian seasoning
2 tablespoons minced garlic
1 cup sun-dried tomatoes, chopped
1¼ to 1½ cups fresh Parmesan cheese, finely grated
3 tablespoons olive oil, divided
1 tablespoon flour
½ cup white wine (Pinot Grigio)
6 oz. bag baby spinach
2 cups light cream
Salt and pepper, to taste
1 lb. farfalle pasta

~A Day Ahead~

Rinse the chicken and pat them dry with paper towels. Season the chicken with salt, pepper, and Italian seasoning. Place the chicken in a sealed bag and refrigerate. Mince the garlic and chop the sun-dried tomatoes. Place them in a container together and refrigerate. Grate the Parmesan cheese, place it in a bag, and refrigerate.

~Cooking Directions~

Preheat the oven to 400°F. Heat 2 tablespoons of oil in a large nonstick skillet over medium-high heat. Add half of the chicken to the pan and brown on both sides. Transfer the chicken to a large sheet pan in a single layer. Brown the second batch of chicken tenders and add them to the sheet pan. Continue to cook the chicken in the oven for 20 minutes. Cook the pasta as directed on the box, drain, and set aside. Meanwhile, in the same skillet over medium heat, add 1 tablespoon of olive oil, the garlic, and the tomatoes. Stir for 1 minute. Add 1 tablespoon of flour. Stir for 1 more minute. Add the wine and mix well. Add the spinach and stir until wilted. Warm the cream in the microwave to room temperature and pour into the skillet. Stir until bubbly. Add the Parmesan cheese and mix well. Return the chicken to the skillet and coat with sauce. Season with salt and pepper, to taste. Serve this over the cooked pasta. Sprinkle grated Parmesan cheese on top if desired. Serves 4 - 5.

Lasagna

Use the Spaghetti Sauce recipe in this book to make this lasagna. Freeze any leftover sauce, meatballs, and sausage for another meal. Prepare the lasagna a day ahead or assemble it and freeze for another day. This makes great leftovers!

Spaghetti Sauce with Meatballs and Sausage
16 oz. box lasagna, cooked
8 oz. Swiss cheese, sliced
8 oz. provolone cheese, sliced
3 cups mozzarella cheese, shredded
½ cup Parmesan cheese, grated

~A Day Ahead~

Lay 12 cooked lasagna sheets on wax paper. Dry them with paper towels, if they are very wet. Coat the bottom of a deep lasagna pan (12 x 9 x 3-inches) with sauce. Lay down 3 lasagna sheets in the pan side-by-side. Spread a thin coating of sauce on top. Lay 3 more lasagna sheets down. Make one mixed layer of sliced meatballs and sliced sausages. Spread a thin layer of sauce on top. Lay down a layer of Swiss cheese. Lay down 3 more sheets of lasagna. Spread a thin coat of sauce on top. Lay down one layer of Provolone cheese. Add 3 more lasagna sheets. Spread a thin layer of sauce on top. Lay down 3 more sheets of lasagna and a thin layer of sauce on top. Sprinkle the top with mozzarella and Parmesan cheese. Cover and refrigerate.

~Cooking Directions~

Remove the lasagna from the refrigerator 30 minutes before baking. Preheat the oven to 350°F. Cover and bake for 30 minutes. Uncover and bake for 30 - 45 minutes until bubbly and the cheese is evenly cooked on top.

~Freezing Directions~

Wrap the uncooked lasagna in plastic wrap and 2 layers of heavy-duty foil. Label and freeze up to 3 months.

*Be sure to thaw out the lasagna at least 24 hours ahead in the refrigerator, before you cook it.

London Broil Strips

A kid-friendly recipe!

1½ lbs. london broil steak
½ cup soy sauce
¼ cup olive oil
¼ cup water
2 tablespoons molasses
1 teaspoon powdered ginger
1 large garlic clove, minced

~A Day Ahead~

Cut the steak against the grain in ¼-inch thin slices. Place the meat in a gallon freezer bag. Mix the rest of the ingredients together in a small bowl and pour in the bag. Seal the bag tightly and refrigerate overnight or freeze for a later time.

~Cooking Directions~

When you are ready to cook the beef, grill or broil for 3 - 5 minutes on each side.

~Freezing Directions~

Freeze the marinated meat in a labeled freezer bag up to 3 months.

Defrost the meat in the refrigerator 24 hours before cooking.

Marinated Steak

A grilling favorite in the summertime!

1½ lbs. steak tip strips or flank steak
⅓ cup less sodium soy sauce
⅓ cup olive oil
¼ teaspoon dried thyme leaves
½ teaspoon black ground pepper
2 large garlic cloves, minced
2 tablespoons ketchup
1 tablespoon brown sugar

~A Day Ahead~

Mix all of the ingredients (except the steak) in a gallon-size freezer bag. Add the steak, seal, and refrigerate. Marinate for 24 hours before cooking or place in the freezer. Serves 4.

~Cooking Directions~

Broil or grill 5 - 8 minutes on each side.

~Freezing Directions~

Freeze the marinated meat in a labeled freezer bag up to 3 months.

If frozen, thaw the meat in the refrigerator for 24 hours before cooking.

Meatballs and Gravy in the Crock-Pot

Just one hour in the Crock-Pot, and you have enough meatballs for several meals! Freeze in desired portions for a quick weeknight meal. Just thaw and reheat in the microwave.

2½ lbs. ground turkey breast

2 lbs. ground beef, 85% lean

2 large eggs

1½ cups Italian-style bread crumbs

3 garlic cloves, minced

1 medium onion, finely chopped

½ teaspoon salt

½ teaspoon black ground pepper

⅓ cup Parmesan cheese, grated

⅓ cup milk

2 (10¾ oz.) cans 45% less sodium cream of mushroom soup

2 cups water

2 envelopes (0.87 oz. each) turkey gravy mix

12 oz. fresh mushrooms, sliced

~Cooking Directions~

Preheat the oven to 350°F. In a large mixing bowl, combine the ground turkey, beef, eggs, bread crumbs, garlic, onion, salt, pepper, cheese, and milk. Using ⅛ cup of meat mixture for each meatball, place the meatballs on a large sheet pan, and cook for 25 minutes. (It's okay if the meatballs overlap on the sheet pan.) Heat a large Crock-Pot on high heat. Mix the soup, water, gravy mix, and mushrooms in the Crock-Pot. Add the meatballs to the Crock-Pot and mix well. Cook on high heat for one hour. Serve with mashed potatoes, rice, or noodles. Makes 76 meatballs.

Meat Pies

One of my childhood favorites that my mom used to make!

2 boxes (15 oz.) refrigerated pie pastry
5 medium potatoes, peeled and sliced
½ teaspoon salt
1¾ lbs. ground beef
1¾ lbs. ground pork
1 medium onion, diced
1¼ teaspoons seasoned salt
1½ teaspoons poultry seasoning

~A Day Ahead~

Remove the pie pastry from the refrigerator, so it can warm up to room temperature. Boil the potatoes with ½ teaspoon of salt until tender, about 20 -25 minutes. Meanwhile, brown the meat and onion in a large skillet over medium heat, stirring occasionally. Drain the meat; set aside. Drain and mash the potatoes with a potato masher. Add the potatoes, seasoned salt, and poultry seasoning to the meat and mix well. Set aside to cool.

Line two pie plates with a pie crust and fill with the meat stuffing evenly. Cover with top crusts and trim the edges with a sharp knife. Seal the edges together by pressing a fork all the way around the rim. Cut a slice in the center of the crust to vent. Cover well with plastic wrap and refrigerate.

~Cooking Directions~

Bake at 400°F for 40 - 45 minutes or until golden brown. Serve hot.

~Freezing Directions~

Wrap the pies in plastic wrap and 2 layers of heavy-duty foil. Label and freeze up to 3 months.

*Be sure to thaw in the refrigerator 24 hours before cooking.

Mini Meatloaves

Mini loaves are convenient to freeze. They take less time to thaw out in the refrigerator.

2 lbs. lean ground beef
½ teaspoon salt
½ teaspoon pepper
1 teaspoon dried minced onion
1 clove of garlic, minced
½ cup Italian-style or garlic & herb bread crumbs
⅓ cup Parmesan cheese, grated
½ cup ketchup
1 large egg

Optional Sauce:
¼ cup ketchup
2 tablespoons light brown sugar
1 teaspoon dry mustard

~A Day Ahead~

In a large mixing bowl, combine the beef, salt, pepper, onion, garlic, bread crumbs, cheese, ketchup, and egg. Press the mixture evenly into four 3 x 5 x 2-inch mini loaf foil pans. Cover and refrigerate.

~Cooking Directions~

Remove the meatloaves from the refrigerator 30 minutes before cooking. Preheat the oven to 350°F. Bake uncovered, for 45 minutes. Combine the sauce ingredients and brush on top of the loaves if desired. Bake for 10 more minutes.

~Freezer Directions~

Wrap the uncooked meatloaves (without the sauce on top) in plastic wrap and place in labeled freezer bags. Freeze up to 3 months.

Thaw the meatloaves in the refrigerator 24 hours before heating. Bake as directed.

Mushroom Burgers

A few extra ingredients turn this burger into a treat!

1 tablespoon olive oil
1 shallot, finely diced
1 cup mushrooms, diced (no stems)
1 garlic clove, minced
1½ lbs. ground beef, 85% lean
½ teaspoon salt
½ teaspoon pepper
4 slices of American, cheddar, or Swiss cheese

~A Day Ahead~

Heat a nonstick skillet over medium-high heat. Add the olive oil and sauté the shallot, mushrooms, and garlic until tender, about 3 - 5 minutes. Cover and cool in the refrigerator. In a large bowl, combine the shallot, mushrooms, garlic, ground beef, salt and pepper. Divide the mixture into 4 equal hamburger patties. Cover and refrigerate until ready to grill or cook in a skillet.

~Cooking Directions~

Grill or cook the burgers in a large skillet over medium heat on both sides until cooked through. Top each burger with a slice of cheese and cook until melted.

~Freezing Directions~

The hamburger patties stay best in the freezer, if you store them in individual vacuum-sealed bags up to 3 months.

Panko Breaded Pork Medallions

A crispy, baked dish the whole family will enjoy!

2 pork tenderloins (1 lb. each)
3 - 4 tablespoons garlic & herb spreadable cheese
2 cups Italian-style panko crispy bread crumbs

~A Day Ahead~

Spray a large sheet pan with nonstick spray; set aside. Rinse the pork under cold water and pat dry with paper towels. Place one pork tenderloin on a large cutting board. Cut 1-inch slice medallions; set aside on a paper towel. Slice the second pork tenderloin in the same manner. Lay all of the pork out on a paper towel, cover with plastic wrap, and pound each piece with a kitchen mallet until all pieces are ¼-inch thin. Using a butter knife, spread a very light coating of the spreadable cheese on each side of the medallions. Roll each slice in the bread crumbs. Place them on the sheet pan. Cover well with plastic wrap and refrigerate.

~Cooking Directions~

Take the pork out of the refrigerator 20 - 30 minutes before cooking. Preheat the oven to 400°F. Uncover the pork, spray the tops of the pork with nonstick spray, and bake for 30 minutes. Serves 6 - 7 people (makes about 14 medallions).

Pork Florentine

Tasty and satisfying!

2 pork tenderloins (1 lb. each)
2 teaspoons olive oil
1 teaspoon Mrs. Dash Garlic & Herb Seasoning Blend

Spinach mixture:
2 tablespoons olive oil
¼ cup onion, diced
1 cup mushrooms, chopped (no stems)
3 garlic cloves, minced
9 or 10 oz. bag of baby spinach
Salt and pepper, to season
½ cup shredded Swiss cheese

~A Day Ahead~

Spray a 12 x 8 x 2-inch baking dish with nonstick spray; set aside. Rinse the pork under cold water and dry with paper towels. Remove as much silver skin on the pork as possible with a sharp knife. Place the pork side-by-side in the baking dish. Cover with plastic wrap and refrigerate.

For the spinach mixture: Heat 2 tablespoons of olive oil in a large nonstick skillet over medium heat. Add the onion and mushrooms and sauté until tender, stirring occasionally. Add the garlic and stir for one minute. Add the spinach, season with salt and pepper, and stir constantly until all the spinach is wilted. Cool the mixture in a bowl, cover, and refrigerate.

~Cooking Directions~

Take the pork out of the refrigerator 30 minutes before cooking. Preheat the oven to 375°F. Uncover the pork. Rub 1 teaspoon of olive oil all over each piece of pork. Sprinkle the pork with Garlic & Herb Seasoning and bake the pork (without the spinach mixture) for 1 hour. When the hour is up, spread the spinach mixture around the pork and sprinkle with Swiss cheese. Bake 15 minutes longer. Serves 5.

Prosciutto Wrapped Stuffed Chicken

I recommend assembling these delicious bundles a day ahead. Then all you need to do is bake them the next day!

2 tablespoons olive oil
¼ cup onion, finely diced
1 cup mushrooms, sliced (no stems)
3 garlic cloves, minced
9 oz. baby spinach
¼ cup sun-dried tomatoes, chopped
4 boneless, skinless chicken breasts
Salt and pepper, to season
¾ cup Swiss cheese, shredded
4 thin slices prosciutto
4 teaspoons of olive oil

~Cooking Directions~

Heat 2 tablespoons of olive oil in a large skillet over medium heat. Sauté the onion and mushrooms until tender. Add the garlic and spinach. Stir until the spinach is wilted. Stir in the tomatoes and cook for 1 minute. Transfer the spinach mixture to a bowl, cover, and refrigerate. Pound the chicken to ¼-inch thickness. Season the chicken with salt and pepper. Spread the spinach mixture evenly on each chicken breast. Sprinkle with Swiss cheese. Roll up the chicken. Place each chicken roll on a slice of prosciutto. Wrap the prosciutto around the chicken and secure it with 2 toothpicks. Cross the toothpicks like an "X" so they stay secure. Place the chicken bundles seam-side down in a baking dish sprayed with nonstick spray. Cover tightly and refrigerate.

~The Next Day~

Take the chicken dish out of the refrigerator 30 minutes before cooking. Preheat the oven to 400°F. Drizzle one teaspoon of olive oil over each chicken bundle. Bake uncovered for 30 - 35 minutes, or until juices run clear when tested with a knife. Serves 4.

Sausage Calzones

An easy, weeknight meal for the family or for a football party!

1 lb. breakfast or Italian turkey sausage
2 tablespoons olive oil
2 green bell peppers, sliced
2 onions, sliced
Salt and pepper, to taste
8 oz. ball of fresh mozzarella cheese
2 refrigerated packages of prepared pizza dough
Flour, for dusting
1 egg white
2 tablespoons water

~A Day Ahead~

Heat a large nonstick skillet over medium heat. Remove the casings from the sausage. Brown the sausages, breaking them apart with a spoon as they cook. Drain the sausage and set aside to cool. Meanwhile, heat the olive oil in another large skillet over medium heat and cook the peppers and onions with the salt and pepper until tender. (You may need to turn the heat down to medium-low, so the vegetables don't brown too fast.) Place the sausage, peppers, and onions in a covered container and store in the refrigerator, until you're ready to cook the calzones. Slice the mozzarella cheese into ¼-inch slices. Cover and store the cheese in the refrigerator.

~Cooking Directions~

Remove the pizza dough and the container of sausage and vegetables from the refrigerator 30 minutes before baking. Preheat the oven to 450°F. Dust the counter with some flour. Roll out one batch of pizza dough. Place half of the sausage and half of the vegetables on one half of the dough. Place half of the cheese slices on top. Fold the dough over the sausage, vegetables, and cheese. Wet the inside edge of the dough with a bit of water. Tuck the top dough underneath the bottom dough and press the dough together to seal well. With a sharp knife, cut a small slice in the center of the calzone dough to vent. Combine the egg white with 2 tablespoons of water in a small bowl. Brush the egg wash all over the top of the calzone. Place on a large sheet pan or heated pizza stone. Make the 2nd calzone with the remaining ingredients in the same manner and place on the same sheet pan if possible. Bake for about 12 minutes. Let stand for 5 - 10 minutes before eating. Serves 5.

Sausage Quesadillas

With a little prep ahead, this will be on the table in no time!

2 lbs. turkey breakfast or Italian sausages, casings removed
1 red bell pepper, sliced
1 green bell pepper, sliced
1 medium onion, sliced
4 tablespoons cream cheese
8 ten-inch flour tortillas
16 oz. Monterey Jack cheese, shredded
1 cup corn (optional)

~A Day Ahead~

In a large nonstick pan, break up the sausages into pieces and brown them with the peppers and onions until cooked through. Drain and transfer the sausage, peppers, and onions to a bowl to cool. Cover and refrigerate, until you are ready to make the quesadillas.

~Cooking Directions~

Remove the sausage container from the refrigerator 30 minutes before cooking. Preheat the oven to 350°F. Place 2 tortillas side by side on a large sheet pan. Spread each tortilla with 1 tablespoon of cream cheese. Spread ¼ of the sausage mixture on each tortilla. Add your desired amount of cheese and corn. Top each with a tortilla. Bake for 10 minutes. Make 2 more quesadillas in the same manner and bake. Cut each quesadilla into wedges and serve immediately with sour cream on the side. This makes 4 large quesadillas that will feed 4 - 6 people.

Shepherd's Pie

An oldie but a goodie!

1 lb. ground beef, 85% lean
¼ cup onion, diced
¼ teaspoon salt
¼ teaspoon black ground pepper
2 lbs. potatoes (about 4 medium), peeled and sliced
½ cup chive and onion cream cheese (reduced fat)
1 tablespoon butter
1 tablespoon milk
¼ teaspoon black ground pepper
14.5 oz. can creamed corn

~A Day Ahead~

In a large skillet over medium heat, brown the beef and the onion together. Drain well and season with salt and pepper. Place the beef mixture in a 9 x 9 x 2-inch baking dish. Set aside to cool. Meanwhile, boil the potatoes in a medium pan for 20 - 25 minutes. Drain the potatoes and place them in a large mixing bowl. Add the cream cheese, butter, milk, and pepper. Mix on medium speed until smooth. Pour the creamed corn evenly over the beef mixture. Spread the mashed potatoes evenly over the corn. When the potatoes have cooled, cover with foil and refrigerate until ready to bake.

~Cooking Directions~

Remove the dish from the refrigerator 30 minutes before baking. Preheat the oven to 350°F. Uncover and bake for 35 - 40 minutes, or until the corn is bubbly around the sides. Serves 4.

Sloppy Joes

This recipe freezes very well. Keep some in the freezer for a quick meal. All you have to do is defrost and reheat it in the microwave.

2 lbs. ground beef, 85% lean
2 celery ribs, finely diced
⅔ cup onion, finely diced
⅔ cup green bell pepper, finely diced
½ cup ketchup
½ cup Bull's-Eye Original Barbecue Sauce
16 oz. tomato sauce
2 tablespoons light brown sugar, packed
2 teaspoons dry mustard
2 tablespoons Worcestershire sauce
2 tablespoons vinegar
Salt and pepper, to taste
8 hamburger buns

~A Day Ahead~

In a large skillet, cook the beef, celery, onion, and green pepper on medium heat, until the beef is cooked through. Drain the fat. Add the ketchup, barbecue sauce, tomato sauce, brown sugar, mustard, Worcestershire sauce, vinegar, salt, and pepper. Cover and simmer for 15 minutes, stirring occasionally. Transfer the mixture to a bowl to cool. Cover and refrigerate until ready to reheat.

~Cooking Directions~

Reheat in the microwave. Serve on hamburger buns. Makes 8 sloppy joes.

~Freezing Directions~

Freeze the sloppy joes in labeled freezer bags and freeze flat. This defrosts in the microwave very quickly for an easy weeknight meal.

Spaghetti Sauce

I have tested so many spaghetti sauce recipes over the years. I am finally happy with this one. I use this sauce with Chicken Parmesan, Baked Manicotti, and Lasagna.

Sauce:

2 tablespoon olive oil

⅔ cup onion, diced

4 to 5 cloves garlic, minced

2 (28 oz.) cans ground peeled tomatoes

2 (12 oz.) cans tomato paste

2¾ cups water

2 teaspoons dried oregano

½ teaspoon black ground pepper

2 tablespoons sugar

⅛ teaspoon crushed red pepper flakes (optional)

6 to 8 sweet Italian sausages (not necessary)

+ Salt to taste

Meatballs:

1½ lbs. ground beef, 85% lean

2 eggs

¼ cup milk

½ cup Italian bread crumbs

⅓ cup Parmesan cheese, grated

1 tablespoon dried minced onion

2 cloves garlic, minced

½ teaspoon salt

½ teaspoon pepper

~A Day Ahead~

Preheat the oven to 350°F. In a large bowl, mix all of the meatball ingredients together. Use ¼ cup of the meatball mixture to form a meatball. Place all of the meatballs and sausages on a large broiler pan or sheet pan. Bake 25 minutes.

Meanwhile, heat the oil in a large Dutch oven over medium heat. Add the onion and stir occasionally until translucent. Add the garlic and stir for one more minute. Turn the heat down to medium-low and add the ground tomatoes, tomato paste, water, oregano, pepper, sugar, and pepper flakes. Stir well until smooth. Add the drained meatballs and sausages to the sauce and simmer for 1½ hours. Lower the heat, if the sauce sticks to the bottom of the pan. Stir occasionally.

Cover and refrigerate the sauce, meatballs, and sausage, once they have cooled, and reheat them on the stove or in the microwave the next day.

~Freeze~

This freezes very well for 3 months. Freeze a few batches in labeled plastic containers that seal well.

This defrosts very easily in the microwave.

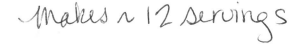
Makes ~ 12 servings

Steak Fajitas

If you're craving a little Mexican food, this should do the trick!

2 lbs. flank steak
¼ cup lime juice
2 tablespoons canola oil
2 large garlic cloves, minced
2 tablespoons lite soy sauce
1 tablespoon ground cumin
2 teaspoons light brown sugar
2 large jalapenos, finely diced
2 medium onions, sliced
2 large green peppers, sliced
2 tablespoons vegetable oil
½ teaspoon salt
½ teaspoon pepper
10 (6-inch) flour tortillas
8 oz. 4-cheese Mexican shredded cheese
8 oz. sour cream

~In the Morning~

Rinse the steak under cold water and pat it dry with paper towels. Place the steak on a cutting board. Cut the steak in half lengthwise. Now cut ¼-inch strips (cutting against the grain). Place the steak in a large bowl. In a small bowl, combine the lime juice, oil, garlic, soy sauce, cumin, brown sugar, and jalapenos. Pour the lime juice mixture over the steak and toss well. Cover and refrigerate until dinnertime. Place the sliced onions and peppers in a separate container and refrigerate.

~At Dinnertime~

Heat the vegetable oil in a large nonstick skillet over medium heat. Add the onions, peppers, salt, and black pepper. Stir occasionally and cook until tender. Remove the onions and peppers and place in a bowl. Brown the steak on both sides in the hot skillet in 3 or 4 batches on medium-high heat. Add additional oil to the pan if necessary. When all of the steak is cooked, return all of the steak and vegetables to the pan and mix together. Turn the heat down to low and keep warm.

~Assembling the Fajitas~

Place a damp paper towel on a dinner plate. Put the stack of tortillas on top. Place another damp paper towel over it. Microwave the tortillas for 20 seconds on high power. Take one tortilla at a time and add ½ cup of the steak and vegetables on the tortilla. Add some shredded cheese and sour cream. Roll up the fajitas and serve immediately. Makes 10 fajitas.

Stuffed Beef Tenderloin

Beef tenderloin is very expensive, so this is a special treat in my family. The beef is so tender and the flavor is out of this world!

5 - 6 lbs. beef tenderloin (½ lb. per person)
2 garlic cloves, minced (to rub all over the beef)
Salt and black ground pepper (to season the outside of the beef)

Stuffing:
1 cup water
1 lb. fresh spinach
2 tablespoons butter
8 oz. fresh mushrooms, chopped (no stems)
2 garlic cloves, minced
1¼ cups Swiss cheese, shredded
1 large egg
½ teaspoon salt
½ teaspoon black ground pepper

~A Day Ahead~

Prepare the stuffing: In a large saucepan with 1 cup of water, boil the spinach until wilted. Drain and chop the spinach; set aside. Melt the butter in a large nonstick skillet over medium heat. Cook the mushrooms until tender, about 4 - 5 minutes. Add the spinach and garlic and stir for 2 minutes. Remove this mixture to a medium bowl to cool. Stir in the cheese, egg, salt, and pepper. Cover and refrigerate until you are ready to cook the beef.

~Cooking Directions~

Rinse the beef under cold water and pat dry with paper towels. Cut a lengthwise pocket into the side of the beef and fill with the stuffing. Tie the beef tightly with 5 or 6 separate strings to keep the pocket closed. Cut off the excess strings if they're hanging. Rub the outside of the beef with the minced garlic and season with salt and pepper. Insert a cooking thermometer in the thickest part of the beef (not the stuffing). Grill on a rotisserie or cook in the oven at 375°F, until the thermometer registers rare in the center. Do not overcook. The ends will be more done. Let the beef rest for 15 minutes before you cut it. Remove the strings. Cut into ½-inch slices.

Note: This type of beef is less expensive at your local wholesale club.

Stuffed Cornish Hens

There's something special about having your own little Cornish hen to yourself!

1½ tablespoons butter
3 tablespoons onion, finely diced
½ cup celery, finely diced
½ of a giant loaf of white bread
½ tablespoon Bell's Poultry Seasoning
¼ teaspoon salt
¼ teaspoon black ground pepper
2½ cups low sodium chicken broth
6 Cornish hens (one Cornish hen per person)
2 - 3 tablespoons canola oil
Mrs. Dash Chicken Grilling Seasoning, to taste

~A Day Ahead~

In a small skillet, melt the butter over medium heat. Add the onion and celery and sauté until lightly brown; set aside. Toast the bread on a large sheet pan under the broiler. Be sure to toast both sides. Tear up the toast into bite-size pieces and place them in a large bowl. Add the onion, celery, poultry seasoning, salt, pepper, and broth. Stir the stuffing until well combined. Cover the stuffing and refrigerate overnight.

~Cooking Directions~

Remove the bread stuffing from the refrigerator 30 minutes before cooking. Preheat the oven to 400°F. Clean the hens, inside and out, under cold running water. Pat them dry with paper towels, inside and out. Place the hens on a large baking pan. Brush them lightly with canola oil. Sprinkle each with Grilling Seasoning. Stuff each hen with ½ cup of bread stuffing. Bake for 70 minutes. Let the hens stand for 10 - 15 minutes before serving.

Taco Lasagna

You can prepare this a day ahead and cook it for dinner the next day, or you can prepare the lasagna and freeze it.

9 lasagna sheets (cook a few extra just in case)
1 lb. ground beef, 85% lean
1 lb. ground turkey breast
4 tablespoons dried minced onion
4 teaspoons chili powder
1½ teaspoons dried basil
2 teaspoons dried oregano
2 teaspoons garlic powder
¾ teaspoon salt
1 teaspoon black ground pepper
2 teaspoons ground cumin
¼ teaspoon ground cayenne red pepper
1¼ cups water
2¼ cups mild or medium thick salsa
2 cups Mexican taco cheese, shredded
8 oz. sour cream (to serve with the lasagna)

~A Day Ahead~

Cook the lasagna according to the directions on the box. Drain the pasta and lay the sheets out on wax paper or plastic wrap. Meanwhile, brown the meat in a large skillet on medium heat. Drain the fat and reduce the heat to medium-low. Stir in the onion, chili powder, basil, oregano, garlic powder, salt, pepper, cumin, cayenne pepper, and water. Simmer and stir until the mixture thickens; remove from heat.

Spray a 9 x 14 x 2-inch baking dish with nonstick spray. Lay 3 sheets of lasagna lengthwise in the dish. Spread ¾ cup of salsa over the lasagna. Lay down 3 more sheets of lasagna. Spread all of the taco meat mixture evenly on top. Sprinkle 1 cup of the cheese, lay another 3 sheets of lasagna, spread 1½ cups salsa over it, and sprinkle 1 cup of cheese on top. Cover the dish and refrigerate.

~Cooking Directions~

Remove the lasagna from the refrigerator 30 minutes before cooking. Preheat the oven to 375°F. Cover and bake for 20 minutes. Uncover and bake for 20 - 25 minutes or until bubbly. Serve with sour cream on the side.

~Freezing Directions~

Wrap in 2 layers of plastic wrap and 2 layers of heavy-duty aluminum foil. Label and freeze up to 3 months.

Taco Pie

Some people like to serve cornbread on the side. Try the cornbread on top and make it a one-dish meal!

2½ lbs. ground beef, 85% lean
½ cup green bell pepper, diced
½ cup red bell pepper, diced
1 large jalapeno pepper, finely diced
2 packets (1.25 oz. each) taco seasoning
1½ cups water
1 cup frozen corn

Cornbread topping:
2 pouches (6.5 oz. each) cornbread & muffin mix
⅔ cup milk
4 tablespoons butter, melted
2 large eggs

~A Day Ahead~

In a large skillet over medium-high heat, cook the beef and peppers, until the beef is completely browned. Drain the fat. Reduce the heat to medium-low and add the taco seasoning and water. Stir until well combined and thickened. Remove from heat and stir in the corn. Spray a 9 x 14 x 2-inch baking dish with nonstick spray. Pour the taco meat into the dish and spread evenly. Cool, cover, and refrigerate.

~Cooking Directions~

Remove the taco meat from the refrigerator 30 minutes before cooking. Preheat the oven to 375°F. In a medium bowl, mix the cornbread mix, milk, melted butter, and eggs. Unwrap the taco dish and pour the cornbread batter over the taco meat evenly. (If the batter doesn't spread to the edge, it's okay. It will spread more when it cooks.) Bake for 25 minutes or until a toothpick inserted in the center of the cornbread comes out clean. Serve with sour cream on the side. Serves 6.

Tacos

This is a great recipe to cook and freeze. You can defrost and heat it in the microwave for a quick weeknight meal.

2 lbs. ground beef
4 tablespoons dried minced onion
4 teaspoons chili powder
1½ teaspoons dried basil
2 teaspoons dried oregano
2 teaspoons garlic powder
¾ teaspoon salt
1 teaspoon ground black pepper
2 teaspoons ground cumin
¼ teaspoon ground cayenne red pepper
1¼ cup water
10 to 12 flour tortillas (taco size)

Toppings:
1 plum tomato, chopped
Lettuce, shredded
Cheddar cheese, shredded
8 oz. sour cream

~A Day Ahead~

In a large skillet, brown the ground beef on medium heat. Break up the larger pieces of beef with a spoon and turn occasionally until no longer pink. Drain the fat and reduce the heat to medium-low. Stir in the minced onion, chili powder, basil, oregano, garlic powder, salt, pepper, cumin, cayenne pepper, and water. Simmer and stir until the mixture thickens; remove from heat. Place the taco meat in a covered container and refrigerate.

~Cooking Directions~

Reheat the taco meat in the microwave. To make the tortillas more pliable, place the stack of tortillas between damp paper towels and place in the microwave for 10 - 20 seconds on high. Fill each tortilla with ½ cup of meat mixture and your favorite toppings.

~Freezing Directions~

After cooking the taco meat mixture, place it in a covered container and cool it completely in the refrigerator. Place the taco mixture in labeled freezer bags. Freeze up to 3 months. Defrost in the microwave and heat through for a quick meal. Makes about 12 tacos.

Teriyaki Chicken

This is one of those meals I like to keep on hand in the freezer.

1 tablespoon cornstarch
2 teaspoons water
¼ cup sugar
¼ cup light brown sugar, packed
½ cup less sodium soy sauce
¼ cup cider vinegar
¼ cup fresh orange juice
1 teaspoon garlic powder
½ teaspoon ground ginger
8 - 10 skinless, boneless chicken thighs

In a gallon freezer bag, combine all of the ingredients except the chicken. Mix thoroughly. Add the chicken and seal. Refrigerate up to 24 hours before cooking or freeze in a labeled freezer bag up to 3 months.

~Cooking Directions~

Remove the chicken from the refrigerator 30 minutes before cooking. Preheat the oven to 350°F. Place the chicken and all of the liquid in a 13 x 9 x 2-inch baking dish (uncovered). Bake for 30 minutes, turn the pieces over, and bake for 30 more minutes. This chicken can also be grilled on medium heat about 12 -14 minutes on each side. It is done when the juice runs clear. Serves 4 - 5.

Thai Chicken Thighs

This recipe has a lot of flavor, whether you marinate it one hour or overnight. It's your choice!

8 boneless, skinless chicken thighs
1 tablespoon fresh ginger, finely grated
1 tablespoon garlic, minced
1 tablespoon fish sauce
1 tablespoon light brown sugar
1½ tablespoons lower sodium soy sauce
1½ tablespoons olive oil
2 tablespoons fresh basil, chopped
2 tablespoons fresh cilantro, chopped
1 or 2 jalapenos, finely diced (optional)

~A Day Ahead~

Add all of the ingredients, except the chicken, to a gallon-size freezer bag. Mix thoroughly. Add the chicken and seal. Turn the bag carefully, so that all of the chicken gets coated with the marinade. Refrigerate up to 24 hours before cooking, or label and freeze for another time.

~Cooking Directions~

Grill on medium heat or broil on the upper middle rack for 12 - 14 minutes on each side. Serves 4.

Tuna Noodle Casserole

A delicious classic for the family or for a potluck dinner!

4 cups wide egg noodles
1 tablespoon butter
2 cups fresh mushrooms, sliced (no stems)
1 shallot, diced
Salt and pepper, to taste
2 garlic cloves, minced
1 tablespoon flour
1 cup whole milk (warmed to room temperature)
½ cup heavy cream (warmed to room temperature)
⅓ cup frozen petite peas
½ cup freshly grated Parmesan cheese (Parmigiano-Reggiano)
12 oz. can solid white albacore tuna, drained
Topping: ¼ cup Parmesan cheese, grated

~A Day Ahead~

Spray a 13 x 9 x 2-inch baking dish with nonstick spray; set aside. Cook the noodles according to the directions on the package; drain and set aside. In a large skillet over medium heat, melt the butter and sauté the mushrooms and shallot for about 6 - 8 minutes. Season with salt and pepper. Add the garlic and flour and stir for 1 minute. Add the milk and cream. Stir constantly, until it thickens. Remove the pan from the heat. Add the peas, ½ cup of cheese, tuna, and noodles. Season with salt and pepper and mix gently. Pour the noodle mixture evenly into the baking dish. Sprinkle ¼ cup of Parmesan cheese on top. Set aside and cool. Cover the casserole and refrigerate.

~Cooking Directions~

Remove the casserole from the refrigerator 30 minutes before cooking. Preheat the oven to 350°F. Cover and bake for 30 minutes. Uncover and broil for 5 minutes, on the middle rack, to get the top a little crunchy. Serves 6.

Turkey Burgers

Freeze the burgers individually and grill or broil, at your convenience, for a quick and healthy meal!

1.3 lbs. ground breast of turkey
1 egg, lightly beaten
½ cup Gruyere cheese, finely grated
¼ to ⅓ cup scallions, thinly sliced
⅓ cup Italian style bread crumbs
1 tablespoon spicy brown mustard
3 garlic cloves, minced
½ teaspoon salt
½ teaspoon pepper

Mix all of the ingredients together in a large bowl. For each burger, use ½ cup of the turkey mixture. Make 5 burger patties and wrap them individually in plastic wrap. Place the burgers in a labeled freezer bag and freeze up to 3 months.

Defrost the burgers in the microwave before cooking. Grill, broil, or fry in a bit of olive oil. Melt your favorite cheese on top. Serve on a toasted hamburger bun. Optional toppings: lettuce, sliced tomato, or pickles.

Side Dishes

Baked Beans

Broccoli Salad

Carrot and Broccoli Casserole

Carrot Casserole

Chive and Onion Potato Casserole

Hawaiian Coleslaw

Healthy Broccoli Slaw

Italian Sub Salad

Layered Cheesy Zucchini

Macaroni and Cheese

Macaroni Salad

Mashed Potato Casserole

Potato Salad

Stir-Fried Asparagus

Strawberry Spinach Salad

Taco Salad

Zucchini Parmesan

Zucchini Squares

Baked Beans

Not your average baked beans!

1 medium onion, chopped
3 lbs. ground beef, 85% lean
4 cans (1 lb. each) Original B & M Baked Beans
2 cups ketchup
½ cup molasses
¼ cup white vinegar
¼ cup Worcestershire sauce

~A Day Ahead~

In a large frying pan, cook the onion and beef on medium heat until cooked through; drain the fat. Add the rest of the ingredients and mix well. Pour the mixture into a large, deep casserole dish. Cover and refrigerate.

~Cooking Directions~

Remove the casserole dish from the refrigerator 30 minutes before cooking. Preheat the oven to 350°F. Cover and bake for 35 - 45 minutes or until bubbly. Serves 8 - 10.

Broccoli Salad

A wonderful salad in the summertime!

½ lb. bacon, cut into ½-inch pieces
2 heads of broccoli
¼ cup onion, diced
½ cup dry-roasted peanuts
½ cup raisins

Dressing:
1 cup mayonnaise
¼ cup sugar
1 tablespoon vinegar

~A Day Ahead~

In a large skillet, brown the bacon until crispy. Drain and cool on paper towels. Rinse and cut the broccoli into bite-size pieces. In a medium bowl, add the bacon, broccoli, onions, peanuts, and raisins. Cover and refrigerate. In a small bowl, mix the mayonnaise, sugar, and vinegar. Cover and refrigerate.

~Several Hours before Serving~

Pour the dressing over the broccoli mixture, mix well, and refrigerate. Serves 6.

Carrot and Broccoli Casserole

A delicious family favorite that is perfect for a buffet!

6 carrots, sliced
5 cups broccoli florets, bite size
3 tablespoons olive oil
½ cup Romano cheese, grated
1½ teaspoons garlic powder
¼ teaspoon salt
½ teaspoon ground black pepper
¾ cup Italian-style bread crumbs
1 cup mozzarella cheese, shredded

~A Day Ahead~

Boil the sliced carrots in a 2-quart saucepan for 5 minutes. Add the broccoli and cook for 4 more minutes. Drain and place the vegetables in a 13 x 9 x 2-inch baking dish. Drizzle the olive oil over the vegetables and mix well. Add the cheese, garlic powder, salt, pepper, and bread crumbs. Mix thoroughly. Top with mozzarella cheese. Cover and refrigerate.

~Cooking Directions~

Remove the dish 30 minutes before cooking. Preheat the oven to 350°F. Cover and bake for 20 - 30 minutes or until heated through. Serves 6.

Carrot Casserole

A tasty way to get your family to eat their vegetables!

4 cups carrots, sliced
3 tablespoons butter
1 medium onion, diced
1 cup cheddar cheese, shredded
10.75 oz. cream of celery soup
⅛ teaspoon ground black pepper

Topping:
3 cups crushed herb-seasoned croutons
5 tablespoons butter, melted

~A Day Ahead~

Cook the sliced carrots in boiling water for 10 minutes; drain well. In a small skillet over medium heat, melt the 3 tablespoons of butter and cook the onions until tender. In a 2-quart casserole dish, mix the carrots, onions, cheese, soup, and black pepper. In a medium bowl, mix the croutons with the melted butter and sprinkle over the casserole. Cover and refrigerate.

~Cooking Directions~

Remove the casserole from the refrigerator 30 minutes before cooking. Preheat the oven to 350°F. Uncover and bake for 30 minutes or until bubbly. Serves 4.

Chive and Onion Potato Casserole

More flavorful than ordinary mashed potatoes!

3 lbs. russet potatoes, peeled and sliced
¾ cup chive and onion cream cheese (reduced fat)
2 tablespoons butter
3 tablespoons milk
¼ teaspoon pepper
1 cup cheddar cheese, shredded

~A Day Ahead~

Spray an 8 x 8 x 2-inch baking dish with nonstick spray; set aside. In a medium saucepan, boil the potatoes for about 25 minutes. Drain the potatoes and place in a large mixing bowl. Add the cream cheese, butter, milk, and pepper. Mix on medium speed until smooth and well blended. Pour the mixture into the baking dish. Top evenly with cheese. Cover and refrigerate.

~Cooking Directions~

Remove the casserole from the refrigerator 30 minutes before heating. Preheat the oven to 350°F. Uncover and bake for 30 - 40 minutes. Serves 5 - 6.

Hawaiian Coleslaw

Try this unique, flavorful side dish at your next barbecue.

½ cup mayonnaise
¼ cup Hawaiian marinade with tropical fruit juices
1 can (8 oz.) crushed pineapple in natural juice, undrained
1 package (1 lb.) shredded coleslaw mix
¼ cup raisins
¼ cup dried cranberries
½ cup pecans, chopped

~A Day Ahead~

In a small bowl, combine the mayonnaise, Hawaiian marinade, and pineapple. Cover and refrigerate. In a medium serving bowl, add the coleslaw mix, raisins, cranberries, and pecans. Cover and refrigerate.

~Just Before Serving~

Add the mayonnaise mixture to the coleslaw; mix well. Keep refrigerated until ready to serve. Serves 6.

Healthy Broccoli Slaw

Crunchy, healthy, and delicious!

1 bag (12 oz.) broccoli cole slaw
¾ cup sweetened dried cranberries
¼ to ⅓ cup soy nuts
¼ cup light mayonnaise
1 tablespoon sugar
1½ teaspoons vinegar

~A Day Ahead~

In a medium serving bowl, combine the broccoli, cranberries, and soy nuts. Cover and refrigerate. In a small bowl, combine the mayonnaise, sugar, and vinegar. Cover and refrigerate.

~Just Before Serving~

Add the mayonnaise mixture to the broccoli bowl and mix well. Serves 4 - 5.

Italian Sub Salad

If you like Italian submarine sandwiches, you'll love this salad! It's a great summer side dish.

1 lb. Campanelle or Rotini pasta, cooked and drained
½ to 1 cup dill pickles, cut into ½-inch cubes
½ lb. American cheese, cut into ½-inch cubes
½ lb. boiled ham, cut into ½-inch cubes
1 small onion, diced
1 small green pepper, diced
3 tablespoons red wine vinegar
½ cup vegetable oil
Salt and pepper, to taste

~A Day Ahead~

Mix all of the ingredients together in a large bowl. Cover and keep refrigerated. Serves 6 - 8.

Layered Cheesy Zucchini

If you like zucchini, this is the perfect side dish to bring to a potluck dinner.

1 teaspoon olive oil
5 medium zucchini
8 oz. shredded pizza 4 cheese (mozzarella, provolone, Parmesan & Romano)
½ cup garlic & herb seasoned bread crumbs

~A Day Ahead~

Coat the bottom of an 11 x 8 x 2-inch baking dish with oil. Wash and dry the zucchini. Cut off both ends. Cut all of the zucchini into ¼-inch round slices. Lay down one flat layer of zucchini in the dish. Sprinkle with ½ cup of the cheese. Sprinkle the cheese with 2 tablespoons of the bread crumbs. Repeat this process (a layer of zucchini, cheese, and bread crumbs) until you run out of ingredients. You should end up with the bread crumbs on top. Cover and refrigerate.

~Cooking Directions~

Remove the dish 30 minutes before cooking. Preheat the oven to 350°F. Uncover and bake for about 45 minutes until lightly browned and bubbly. Serves 6.

Macaroni and Cheese

Creamy, cheesy comfort food at its best!

16 oz. box large elbow pasta
6 cups whole milk
½ cup butter
2 tablespoons instant chicken bouillon powder
½ cup flour
1¼ cups sharp cheddar cheese, shredded
1¼ cups American cheese, shredded
½ cup freshly grated Parmesan cheese

~A Day Ahead~

Spray a 13 x 9 x 2-inch baking dish with nonstick spray; set aside. Cook the pasta as directed on the box; drain and set aside. Warm the milk in the microwave to room temperature; set aside. Melt the butter in a large skillet over medium heat. Add the bouillon and flour and whisk for one minute. Slowly whisk in the milk and continue stirring, until there are no lumps and the sauce has thickened. Stir in the cheddar and American cheese and remove from heat. Continue stirring until the cheese has melted. Stir in the cooked pasta until well combined. Pour the macaroni and cheese into the baking dish evenly. Sprinkle the top with Parmesan cheese. Cool for 15 minutes, cover with aluminum foil, and refrigerate.

~Cooking Directions~

Remove the dish from the refrigerator 30 minutes before cooking. Preheat the oven to 350°F. Cover and bake for 30 minutes. Remove the foil and bake another 10 - 15 minutes until bubbly. Serves 6.

Macaroni Salad

A wonderful summer salad to bring to a barbecue!

3 cups elbow or pasta ruffles

½ cup mayonnaise

2 tablespoons Dijon mustard

1¼ cups bread and butter pickles, drained and chopped

1 cup celery, diced

1 scallion, thinly sliced

¼ cup shredded carrot

~A Day Ahead~

Cook the pasta according to the directions on the box. Drain and rinse under cold water. Place in a medium-size serving bowl. Add the rest of the ingredients, mix well, and refrigerate. Serves 5.

Mashed Potato Casserole

A super-fast side dish!

8 oz. cream cheese or Neufchatel cheese, softened
1 cup French onion dip (refrigerated)
2 eggs, beaten
1 cup 1% milk
2 cups water
½ cup margarine
3 cups instant mashed potato flakes

~A Day Ahead~

Spray a 12 x 8 x 2-inch baking dish with nonstick spray; set aside. In a large mixing bowl, beat the cream cheese, onion dip, eggs, and milk until smooth. In a medium saucepan, combine the water and margarine. Bring to a boil and remove from heat. Add the instant potato flakes; mix well. Pour the instant potatoes into the cream cheese mixture. Beat on medium speed until smooth. Pour into the baking dish evenly. Cool, cover, and refrigerate.

~Cooking Directions~

Remove the casserole from the refrigerator 30 minutes before cooking. Preheat the oven to 350°F. Uncover and bake for 30 - 40 minutes. Serves 6.

Potato Salad

The perfect side dish for barbecued chicken, hot dogs, or hamburgers!

3 lbs. red potatoes, washed
¼ teaspoon salt
5 eggs
½ cup Miracle Whip salad dressing
1 tablespoon red onion, minced
¼ cup celery, finely diced
1½ tablespoon fresh parsley, chopped
Salt and pepper, to taste

~A Day Ahead~

Cut the potatoes into quarters. Place them in a large saucepan. Fill the pan with almost enough water to cover the potatoes. Add salt to the water. Bring to a boil on high heat. Then reduce to medium heat until the potatoes are tender, about 15 minutes. Drain the potatoes and place on paper towels to cool. In a separate pan, add the eggs and enough water to nearly cover the eggs. Bring to a boil on high heat. Then reduce to medium-high for 14 minutes. Drain the water. Cover the eggs with cold water to cool. Remove the egg shells. Slice the eggs and place in a medium bowl with the potatoes. Add the salad dressing, onion, celery, parsley, and salt & pepper to taste. Mix well and refrigerate. Serves 6.

Stir-Fried Asparagus

A healthy, crisp-tender vegetable dish!

2 bunches of asparagus
1 plum tomato, cut into ½-inch pieces
4 garlic cloves, sliced
2 tablespoons olive oil
⅛ teaspoon red pepper flakes (optional)
Salt and black ground pepper, to taste

~A Day Ahead~

Rinse and dry the asparagus with paper towels. Cut off and discard the tough dry ends. Cut the asparagus into 1-inch pieces. Cover and store in the refrigerator. Place the tomato pieces and garlic slices in separate containers and refrigerate.

~Cooking Directions~

Heat the oil in a large nonstick skillet over medium heat. Add the garlic and stir occasionally for 3 - 4 minutes. Add the asparagus, tomato, red pepper flakes, salt, and pepper. Stir occasionally for 6 - 8 minutes. Serves 5.

Strawberry Spinach Salad

Light, healthy, and satisfying!

1 lb. spinach, washed with stems removed
2 tablespoon butter
¾ cup sliced almonds
1 pint strawberries, sliced

Dressing:
½ cup sugar
1 tablespoon poppy seeds
2 tablespoon sesame seeds
¼ cup cider vinegar
¼ cup red wine vinegar
½ cup olive oil

~A Day Ahead~

Mix all of the dressing ingredients together in a small bowl. Cover and refrigerate. Rinse the spinach, remove the stems, and spread out on paper towels to dry. Place the spinach in a large serving bowl and refrigerate.

~Just Before Serving~

Melt the butter in a small skillet over medium heat and toast the almonds until light brown. Spread them out on paper towels to cool. Clean and slice the strawberries. Add the strawberries and almonds to the spinach. Pour the dressing over the spinach and mix gently. Serves 5.

Taco Salad

This tasty salad can be served as a side dish or a meal.

1½ lbs. ground beef
1 small green pepper, diced
5 plum tomatoes, diced
12.50 oz. bag of Nacho Cheese Doritos
8 oz. cheddar cheese, shredded
1 head of lettuce, torn into pieces
8 oz. bottle Catalina dressing

~A Day Ahead~

In a large skillet, cook the ground beef on medium heat until cooked through; drain and set aside to cool. Cover and store in the refrigerator. Place the diced green pepper and tomatoes in separate containers and refrigerate. With your hands, crumble the nachos into bite-size pieces and store in a sealed plastic bag at room temperature.

~Just Before Serving~

In a large serving bowl, mix the beef, pepper, tomatoes, cheese, nachos, and torn lettuce. Drizzle enough of the dressing to coat the salad. Toss well. Serves 8 - 10.

Zucchini Parmesan

A nice side dish for an Italian dinner or potluck supper!

4 medium-size zucchini
1 cup Italian-style bread crumbs
1 cup Parmesan cheese, grated
3 eggs
⅓ cup water
2 tablespoons olive oil
2 cups spaghetti sauce
1 cup mozzarella cheese, shredded

~A Day Ahead~

Clean and dry the zucchini. Cut and discard the ends. Cut the zucchini into ¼-inch round slices. Place in a bag and refrigerate. Combine the bread crumbs and Parmesan cheese. Cover and refrigerate.

~Cooking Directions~

Preheat the oven to 350°F. Combine the eggs and water in a shallow bowl. Place the bread crumbs and Parmesan cheese in another shallow bowl. Heat the oil in a large nonstick skillet over medium heat. Dip the zucchini in the egg and coat with the bread crumbs. Brown the zucchini on both sides. You will need to do this in several batches. Add more oil as necessary. Place 2 layers of zucchini in an 11 x 8 x 2-inch baking dish. Put about 6 little dollops of sauce (scattered around) on top of the zucchini. (Don't spread the sauce as it will make the zucchini soggy.) Sprinkle ¼ cup of mozzarella cheese on top. Make 2 more layers of fried zucchini, add the dollops of sauce, and sprinkle another ¼ cup of mozzarella. Place the rest of the zucchini on top, followed by the sauce, and then the rest of the mozzarella cheese. Bake for 30 minutes or until bubbly. Serves 6.

Zucchini Squares

These yummy squares can be served as an appetizer or a side dish.

3 cups zucchini, shredded

⅓ cup onion, finely diced

3 garlic cloves, minced

½ cup Parmesan cheese, grated

½ teaspoon dried oregano

½ teaspoon ground black pepper

2 large eggs

¼ cup canola oil

1 cup Bisquick baking mix

~A Day Ahead~

Spray a 13 x 9 x 2-inch baking dish with nonstick spray; set aside. Spread out the shredded zucchini between several paper towels and press down firmly to remove the excess moisture. Transfer the zucchini to a large bowl. Add the rest of the ingredients and mix well. Pour the mixture into the baking dish evenly. Cover tightly with plastic wrap and refrigerate.

~Cooking Directions~

Remove the baking dish from the refrigerator 30 minutes before baking. Preheat the oven to 350°F. Uncover and bake for 35 - 40 minutes, or until the entire top is lightly browned. A toothpick, inserted in the center, should come out clean. Serve hot. Cut into 12 squares.

Soup

Beef Stew

Cheddar Cheese Soup

Chicken and Spinach Tortellini Soup

Chicken Noodle Soup

Hearty Chili

Italian Wedding Soup

Sausage Lentil Soup

Spicy Corn Chowder

Beef Stew

Comfort food for a cold winter's night!

3 lbs. stew beef, cut into bite-size chunks
1 teaspoon salt
½ teaspoon pepper
2 tablespoons vegetable oil
¼ cup onions, finely diced
⅓ cup flour
10 cups lower sodium beef broth
1 lb. boiling onions, peeled with ends trimmed
5 cups carrots, peeled and sliced
5 large potatoes, peeled and cubed
3 tablespoons flour
½ cup water
Salt and pepper, to taste

Rinse the beef under cold water and pat dry with paper towels. Season with salt and pepper. Heat a large Dutch oven over medium-high heat. Add 2 tablespoons of vegetable oil. Brown the beef in 3 batches and place the cooked beef in a large bowl. Turn the heat down to medium and add ¼ cup of diced onions to the pan. Stir and cook until translucent. Add more oil if necessary. Return the beef to the pan. Sprinkle the beef and onion with ⅓ cup of flour. Stir well until all is coated, about 2 minutes. Add the broth and stir until well combined. Reduce the heat to a simmer. Cook for one hour. Add the carrots and continue cooking for 30 minutes. Add the potatoes and boiling onions and cook 25 minutes longer. In a small bowl, mix 3 tablespoons of flour with ½ cup of water. Stir the stew as you pour in the flour mixture to thicken. Season with salt and pepper, to taste.

~Freeze~

Be sure to cool the stew in the refrigerator before freezing. Freeze in labeled containers up to 3 months.

Cheddar Cheese Soup

This is a great soup for a buffet.

½ lb. lower-sodium bacon, cut into 1-inch pieces
¼ cup butter
1 medium onion, diced
1 green pepper, finely diced
1 red pepper, finely diced
3 large garlic cloves, minced
½ cup flour
2 cups chicken broth
1½ cups whole milk
1½ cups heavy cream
12 oz. block sharp yellow cheddar cheese, shredded
¼ teaspoon Cayenne red pepper (optional)
Salt and white pepper, to taste

~A Day Ahead~

In a large skillet over medium heat, cook the bacon until crispy, stirring occasionally. Place the bacon on several sheets of paper towels to cool and absorb the fat. In a large Dutch oven over medium heat, melt the butter and add the onion and peppers. Sauté for 4 minutes. Add the garlic and stir for 1 minute. Add the flour and stir for 1 minute. Whisk in the broth, milk, and cream. Bring to a boil and immediately turn down the heat to a simmer. Cook for 20 minutes, stirring frequently. Add the cheddar cheese slowly, stirring constantly until melted and smooth. Do not boil, or it will ruin the soup. Stir in the cayenne pepper. Season with salt and white pepper. Pour the soup into a container and refrigerate. Place the bacon in a small container and refrigerate.

~Reheating Directions~

Heat up the soup in the microwave. Top each serving with bacon crumbs if desired.

Chicken and Spinach Tortellini Soup

A quick soup that freezes well!

2 lbs. boneless, skinless chicken breasts
1 tablespoon canola oil
1 shallot, minced
2 garlic cloves, minced
⅛ teaspoon red pepper flakes (optional)
3 quarts low-sodium chicken broth
6 oz. baby spinach
20 oz. chicken & herb tortellini, refrigerated
Salt and pepper, to taste
Grated Parmesan cheese, for serving

Heat the oil in a large Dutch oven over medium-high heat. Brown the chicken breasts on each side. Remove the chicken to a plate. Sauté the minced shallot until tender. Add the garlic and red pepper flakes and stir for one minute. Add the chicken broth and return the chicken to the pot. Season with salt and pepper. Cover and simmer for 25 minutes. Remove the chicken to a plate to cool. Add the spinach and tortellini to the pot and boil for 7 minutes, stirring occasionally. Shred the chicken and add it to the pot. Season with salt and pepper. Serve with grated cheese.

~Freeze~

Cool the soup in the refrigerator before freezing. Freeze the soup in labeled containers up to 3 months.

Chicken Noodle Soup

Everybody needs a classic soup recipe like this.

5½ lbs. cut-up chicken, remove most of the skin
8 cups water
¼ teaspoon poultry seasoning
1 teaspoon salt
½ teaspoon black ground pepper
8 oz. bag celery hearts, sliced
1 lb. carrots, peeled and sliced
1 medium onion, diced
2 garlic cloves, minced
3 cups wide egg noodles, uncooked
3 tablespoons fresh parsley, chopped

In a large Dutch oven, add the chicken, water, poultry seasoning, salt, pepper, celery, carrots, onion, and garlic. Bring to a boil. Then reduce the heat and simmer for 1½ hours. Remove the chicken to a platter to cool. Remove the bones and add the meat back to the pot. In a medium saucepan, boil the noodles for 7 minutes. Drain the noodles and add them to the soup. Add the parsley and season the soup again with salt and pepper. Enjoy some of the soup now and freeze some for later.

~Freeze~

Be sure to cool the soup in the refrigerator before freezing. Freeze the soup in labeled containers up to 3 months.

Hearty Chili

Perfect for a Super Bowl party!

2 lbs. stew beef, cut into bite-size chunks
1 lb. ground pork
¼ cup Worcestershire sauce
5 tablespoons chili powder
¾ teaspoon ground cayenne red pepper
1 teaspoon salt
1 teaspoon cumin
1 tablespoon dried oregano
3 cloves of garlic, minced
2 medium green bell peppers, chopped
2 medium Spanish onions, chopped
3 jalapeno peppers, finely diced
24 oz. can whole tomatoes
16 oz. can tomato sauce
¼ cup white vinegar
½ cup beer
2 (24 oz.) cans red kidney beans
3 cups cheddar cheese, shredded

~A Day Ahead~

Brown the beef and pork in a large Dutch oven over medium heat. Add the Worcestershire sauce, when the meat is halfway cooked. When browned, drain the meat and reserve the liquid. Return the Dutch oven to medium heat and add the rest of the ingredients except the kidney beans, reserved liquid, and cheddar cheese. Bring to a boil. Reduce the heat, cover and simmer for ½ hour, and stir occasionally. Check the consistency of the chili. If more liquid is desired, add some of the reserved liquid. Refrigerate any reserved liquid in case you need it later. Simmer for an additional ½ hour. Remove the Dutch oven from the heat and cool. When cool enough, place the covered Dutch oven in the refrigerator for up to 24 hours.

~Cooking Directions~

When you are ready to heat it up, add the kidney beans and mix well. Simmer until heated through about 25 minutes. Serve with cheddar cheese and soup crackers. Serves 10.

~Freezing Directions~

Be sure the chili is completely cool. Place the chili in labeled containers or freeze flat in labeled freezer bags. Freeze the chili up to 5 months.

Italian Wedding Soup

A quick soup that freezes well!

13 cups lower-sodium chicken broth
1 lb. ground beef
1 lb. ground pork
3 eggs, lightly beaten
¾ cup Italian style bread crumbs
½ teaspoon salt
½ teaspoon black ground pepper
2 teaspoons dried basil
½ teaspoon dried minced garlic
2 teaspoons dried minced onions
½ cup milk
½ cup Parmesan cheese, grated
2 medium escarole, rinsed and chopped (green leaves only)
Additional grated Parmesan cheese, to sprinkle on top of each serving

In a large Dutch oven over high heat, bring the broth to a boil. In a large bowl, mix the beef, pork, eggs, bread crumbs, salt, pepper, basil, garlic, minced onions, milk, and ½ cup of Parmesan cheese. Form ½-inch meatballs and drop into the broth. Add the escarole. Reduce the heat to medium. Cook for 7 minutes. Reduce the heat and simmer for 5 minutes. The soup is done, when all of the meatballs are floating, and the escarole is wilted. Serve the soup with grated Parmesan cheese sprinkled on top.

~Freezing Directions~

Cool the soup completely before freezing. Freeze in labeled containers up to 5 months.

Sausage Lentil Soup

The kielbasa gives this easy soup a little kick.

1 tablespoon olive oil
½ cup onion, diced
4 cups lower sodium chicken broth
4 cups water
1 cup celery, diced
1 lb. lite Polska kielbasa, diced
1½ cups green lentils
1 teaspoon dried marjoram
1 teaspoon dried savory
2 cups carrots, diced
2 cups potatoes, diced
Salt and pepper, to taste

~A Day Ahead~

In a 4-quart pot, heat the olive oil on medium heat. Cook the onion for about 3 – 5 minutes, stirring occasionally. Add the chicken broth, water, celery, sausage, lentils, marjoram, and savory. Bring to a boil. Reduce the heat and simmer for 30 minutes, stirring occasionally. Add the carrots and potatoes and continue simmering for 30 minutes or until the lentils are tender. Season with salt and pepper. Cool and refrigerate.

~Reheating Directions~

Reheat in the microwave or on the stove over medium-low heat.

~Freeze~

Cool the soup completely before freezing. Freeze the soup in labeled containers up to 5 months.

Spicy Corn Chowder

A tasty, thick and spicy soup!

10 cups peeled potatoes, cubed

1 large onion, diced

1 cup green bell pepper, diced

1 cup red bell pepper, diced

4 ham steaks, cubed

½ cup butter

1 teaspoon ground cumin

¼ to ½ teaspoon cayenne red pepper (½ teaspoon has quite a kick!)

⅓ cup flour

2½ cups lower sodium chicken broth (or more if it's too thick)

2 cups milk

2 cans (14.5 oz. each) creamed corn

2½ cups frozen corn

Salt and pepper, to taste

~A Day Ahead~

Peel and cube the potatoes and place them in a container. Cover the potatoes with cold water, cover, and refrigerate. Cut up the onion and peppers. Place them in a container together and refrigerate. Cut the ham into cubes; cover and refrigerate.

~Cooking Directions~

Parboil the potatoes in a large pan for about 10 - 12 minutes. Drain the water and set aside. In a 4-quart pot, melt the butter over medium heat. Sauté the onion and peppers with the cumin and cayenne pepper until tender. Add the flour and whisk for 1 minute. Gradually mix in the broth and milk. Bring to a boil, whisking until smooth. Mix in the creamed corn and frozen corn. Add the ham and potatoes and heat through. Season the chowder with salt and pepper. If the chowder is too thick for you, add more broth and mix well.

~Freezing Directions~

Pour the chowder in freezable containers. Cover and label them. Refrigerate until completely cooled. Freeze up to 3 months.

Measurement Equivalents

Volume Conversions

U.S.	Metric
1 teaspoon	5 mL (milliliter)
2 teaspoons	10 mL
1 tablespoon	15 mL
2 tablespoons	30 mL
¼ cup	59 mL
⅓ cup	79 mL
½ cup	118 mL
¾ cup	177 mL
1 cup	237 mL
1¼ cups	296 mL
1½ cups	355 mL
2 cups	473 mL
2½ cups	592 mL
3 cups	710 mL
4 cups (1 quart)	0.946 L (liter)
1.06 quarts	1 L
4 quarts (1 gallon)	3.8 L

*This conversion chart was rounded to the nearest whole number.

Weight Conversions

Ounces	Grams
½	14
¾	21
1	28
1½	43
2	57
2½	71
3	85
3½	99
4	113
4½	128
5	142
6	170
7	198
8	227
9	255
10	283
12	340
16 (1 pound)	454

*This conversion chart was rounded to the nearest whole number.

Index of Recipes

CPSIA information can be obtained at www.ICGtesting.com
Printed in the USA
269901BV00003B/92/P